Your Names Are Written in Heaven

DAVIDE PERILLO

Your Names Are Written in Heaven

The World of Rose Busingye

Introduction by Julián Carrón
Translated by Matthew Henry

SLANT
BOOKS

YOUR NAMES ARE WRITTEN IN HEAVEN

Copyright © 2025 Davide Perillo. All rights reserved. Except for brief quotations in critical publications or reviews, no part of this book may be reproduced in any manner without prior written permission from the publisher. Write: Permissions, Slant Books, P.O. Box 60295, Seattle, WA 98160.

Slant Books
P.O. Box 60295
Seattle, WA 98160

www.slantbooks.org

Cataloguing-in-Publication data:

Names: Perillo, Davide

Title: Your names are written in heaven: the world of Rose Busingye / Davide Perillo.

Description: Seattle, WA: Slant Books, 2025

Identifiers: ISBN 978-1-63982-182-2 (hardcover) | ISBN 978-1-63982-181-5 (paperback) | ISBN 978-1-63982-183-9 (ebook)

Subjects: LCSH: Missions--Uganda | Non-governmental organizations--Uganda | AIDS (Disease)--Uganda | Catholic Church--Missions

Contents

An Infinite Value by Julián Carrón | vii
Introduction | xiii

   Kireka | 1
   The Point of Departure | 5
   The Encounter | 11
   The Embrace | 23
   AIDS | 29
   The Crisis | 40
   The Women | 46
   The Method | 62
   One by One | 72
   Freedom | 87
   Today and Tomorrow | 99
   The Wave | 112

Notes | 123
Acknowledgments | 125

> What is man that you are mindful of him
> and a son of man that you care for him?
>
> —*Psalm 8*

> I give you back my voice from the womb
> My first cry, it was a joyful noise.
> Only love, only love can leave such a mark
> But only love, only love can heal such a scar.
>
> —U2, *Magnificent*

An Infinite Value

Julián Carrón[1]

ONE OF THE episodes that strikes me most from the life of Rose Businge is what happened to her when she tried to respond to the need of some Ugandan women who were sick with AIDS. She was a nurse in Kampala and had made attempts to help these women, which she explained like this:

> We brought medication to the sick, set them up with treatments. We made charts for them, and they filled them out. But the day after you returned to them, the medicines would be thrown in the trash. And yet they knew what those medicines were for. . . . I thought: "How is this possible? You are sick, you are dying, I bring you medicine that can save your life and you throw it away?"

It was then that something changed in her perception of reality: "I recognized more and more that what I thought was enough was not enough."

This fact did not leave her indifferent. Rather, upon seeing her attempts to help people crumble, for which she had studied and had planned everything she was doing, she was thrown into a profound crisis. "Every day, I saw people die. . . . I got to the point where I wanted to escape. Really: I wanted to go away to a desert island where there were no people. Only insects."

At that moment, she received a phone call from Father Giussani, whom she had met a few years earlier: "Shut down everything and come to Italy." She resisted, but in the end, she gave in and came to Milan, where she spent months visiting Father Giussani frequently. He did nothing but share with her his experience, what he had learned from history.

> One day he said to me: "You know, Rose, a little after the movement started, everyone left. I was alone in the dark, in a tunnel. But at a certain point something happened: I began to say 'I.' And it

was as if a little light started to shine out.... I came out, and at the end of the tunnel, I found three other friends. With those three, the movement started again."

Rose comments: "While he was speaking about the darkness, it was like a replay of my life."

During those weeks in Italy, she discovered Father Giussani: his way of living, of being in reality, of facing daily circumstances. And little by little, Rose observes, sharing life with him "makes you discover yourself." In front of this new awareness of herself, one of the pillars of Father Giussani's human position came to Rose: "The solution to the problems that life poses each day 'does not happen by confronting the problems directly, but by going deeper into the nature of the subject who faces them.' In other words, 'the particular resolves itself by deepening the essential.'"[2] Often, in fact, we take for granted the nature of the subject, and without recognizing it we approach problems according to "a method that in some way reassumes, reabsorbs the cultural tendencies of the world"—that is, in a merely reactive way, a way that lacks cultural originality.

The newness that those months spent with Father Giussani introduced into her way of living soon became clear, as Rose herself remembers:

> I began to live and to work when I knew concretely how to respond to the question "Whose am I?" ... I became free, great because someone had awakened what I am. It was evident that I wasn't nothing; instead I felt embraced and wanted. It was as if his gaze told me: "You ... have an infinite value." From that gaze everything was born. In that gaze, in fact, I discovered that I am not defined by my limits but that the personal relationship with which God makes me exist places in me an infinite desire for him. That gaze of belonging to Christ and to the Church ... established the content and the method of my work: to communicate the feeling for the unlimited greatness of the existence of each person and to offer the same companionship toward destiny that embraces my life.

How many times has Rose reminded us of this over the years! "Father Giussani made me discover my value." And she describes very precisely the reverberation of that gaze on herself: "I felt for the first time an attraction, a love for myself, as if I had never truly looked at myself before. I was taken over by a great tenderness, for me and for everything. I wanted to show to everyone that life has a meaning, that there is a meaning in everything: even in sleeping, in suffering, in dying.... There is a meaning."

It was the discovery of a new world, so much so that it makes her speak about a true and proper "transformation of life: it is you, but it is no longer you. You are something else, something important. If you know it, you treat yourself in a different way." What is more: "You treat things in a different way." Everything is invested with that discovery, as Romano Guardini reminds us: "In the experience of a great love . . . everything that happens becomes an event in its sphere."[3]

And so, we return to the episode of Rose with her women, to the judgment that opened a new way of relating to them: "I understood what was not working in the women, why they did not take their medication." They had not understood their personal value. But in order to discover this for themselves, an explanation, however correct, was not enough. Something else was needed, and she finally understood it: "Giussani continually returned me to my value. He made me discover that. You cannot wait for others to understand it: I am the one who has to discover it. I have to discover Christ the life of my life, in flesh and bones. To discover Jesus within me."

Giussani always pushed her, making her advance step by step, without stopping. And in this emerged his educative genius. She kept putting the problems of her work on the table, and he continually surprised her: "'Don't worry. If your vocation is true, the work will even come out of the rocks.' You remember when Jesus goes to Jerusalem and the Pharisees tell him: 'Make them be quiet, they are causing problems,' and he: 'Even if I made them be quiet, the rocks themselves would cry out'? It was just like that. Giussani told me: 'Let it go, if you are true with your vocation, even if you are shut in a cage, the rocks will begin to sing.'" Rose observes: "Letting go in that case was very difficult: I had my motives, my ideas, my projects. . . . If it were to have happened before those six months with him, I don't know if I would have done it. But after, it was like this: I had nothing but my vocation, the only richness I had in the world. I left that Meeting Point and something else was born, starting from scratch. And to think that after all that I ended up exactly in a place where they break the rocks and sing."

Everything seemed to take its normal course, and yet everything had changed because Rose had changed; her gaze had opened, and her reason broadened. She speaks about herself without reticence: "The things that I said [to the women] were not very different from those I said before. Even before I spoke to the women about their worth, of the importance of what they had around them. I explained to them all the good reasons they had to take care of themselves. But they were explanations. Maybe deep down they were not truly mine." But they became hers.

In time, the difference that she had found surprised the others, to the point that they desired it for themselves. One of her women, raped by rebels from the North, "at a certain point told me: 'For the others I am only a pile of problems; they come and ask me what they did to me, where they took me.... But who am I? I am like a bucket where people throw their trash; but I, as Lucy, who am I?'" Giving her a hug, Rose told her: "Yes, you are all this drama, this disfigured face. But you have an even greater value. You may seem to be only this, but you are worth infinitely more to me." Lucy began to show up at the Meeting Point. "One day she told me: 'Rose, I want to live because you are here. You have given value to my life.' And I answered her: 'No, your value was given to you by Another. Another wants you to exist.'"

An authentic cultural revolution had begun for her and for all those who were around her.

But the story does not end here, and Rose will have to yield again to a reality that is always, stubbornly, greater than her. In order to face the illness of the women, she thinks about opening a hospital. What was a more obvious thing to do? But now the women are the ones to push her, the same ones who were depending on her for their daily needs. They have other priorities: the schools their children attend. "[In those schools] they did not look at our children like human beings. We wanted places that would help them to recognize their value. This is how Rose educated us."

For this reason, in front of Rose's proposal, after a moment of silence, the women who are sick with AIDS respond decisively: "No, not a hospital. We want a school." The priority for them is not a hospital where they can receive care but a school for their children. This new judgment touches on their children, about whom they speak in this way:

> We needed to understand who we are, and we needed to be educated to do it, because it is not revealed automatically. It is for this reason that we have our schools. Even if you get a PhD, in the end you need this awareness of your value. And if while you were studying, they did not teach you this, what use is your PhD? Are you somehow different from the one who stopped at elementary school? We are all equals. There are many people who have everything, have money, live well, have beautiful houses, live in skyscrapers, but are not happy. Because they do not know who they are.

Here is a different gaze, one that reaches everyone. One of Rose's closest collaborators was discouraged because, when she arrived at the nursery school, she found the toys that were bought the day before destroyed. "How does this happen? They are vandals." And Rose: "It is clear that you still have not understood anything. The problem here is not 'rich or poor, black or white.' Teach them that they have value. Here, no one says this to anyone. If they discover that they have a value, you will see that they will know how to value even their toys, their teachers, their classmates. . . ." This new gaze is directed even to the instruments they use. "All this—the projects, the food, anything we use—is the instrument to say to the person: 'You are great, you are greater than you can imagine, you are responsible.' And the projects that we do are like offering a hand to support someone, so that they can take responsibility. We do not say: 'You are nothing, I will feed you, I will do everything for you.'"

Clearly, this is not only a place to get assistance, but a place that makes the self-awareness of the person grow. The sign of change is in the women's perception of themselves as protagonists. At the beginning, they didn't speak to anyone; they had their heads down, without ever raising their eyes, a sign of a total lack of respect for themselves. In time, they begin to dance, to sing, "Now I'm free," to say, "we are here, we have a face."

This freedom penetrates the deepest wounds in their lives. "Many of them," explains Rose, "have undergone and are undergoing injustices: from their husbands, from the rebels. . . . But you see them free. So it means that with everything they have lived—many have been violated, many treated badly and are still treated badly—they have found a justice that is even more just than what we have in mind. They are not imprisoned by their problems, by their poverty, by their illness. Do you remember the woman we came across this morning? That small woman who is always happy. . . ? When I came into her room, the first time, I said to myself: 'O God, she really sleeps here?' She lived in a hole. I asked: Where do your children sleep? 'Here, on the mat.' And she laughed, she didn't complain. But while she said it, I was dying inside. . . . I said to myself: all the complaints that I make are unjust. . . . When it rains, it flows right into their house. And yet she is free, even from injustice. How is this possible?"

Irreducible: this is what Rose and her women are. But in them there is the effort to live up to the situation. Their security is in something else, in something that no one can cause to crumble. Not even the conditions that they have had to face because of Covid have confused them. Rose is certain of it: "One of them, at a certain point, said: 'I realized that if I was hungry I could ask my neighbors for a cup of beans; if I was thirsty there was someone who would give me a glass of water. . . . But life? From whom do I ask for life?'" We have all lived the provocation of the pandemic, but how many of us have been able to ask a question like this? Paradoxically, Covid did not reveal only what was lacking for these people but above all the growth that has happened over these years—if it truly had happened. In Rose's women, it did happen: they did grow, so much so that the newness they experience surprises them first of all. Like the teachers who were challenged by Rose not to lose the best of what happened to them: "You must understand what moved your heart to go and seek out the students. If you lose what happened in your heart, all that you do, all the solutions to these problems, will only last a little while."

What gratitude for this African "flower" that has grown in the field plowed by Father Giussani!

The story told in this book seems to me a cheerful testimony of the "Church that goes out," that Pope Francis never tires of indicating, as the way to respond with life to the unlimited need of people today, who are so in need of the Gospel. Who would not desire to have people like Rose and her women constantly next to them, to go to the ends of the earth and shout to everyone, through the materiality of their own existence, "you have an infinite value"?

Introduction

I DID NOT think I would find what I found in Kampala.

I knew the story of Rose Busingye. I had met her many times on different occasions. We share a friendship and a common path. And I had heard her speak often of herself, of her life and her world. But to go there was another thing.

It was not only the question that always accompanies one as a journalist: to be in person, to encounter people, to enter their world and breathe their air will always be worth much more than reading, or meeting on Zoom, or searching online. There is obviously an abyss between the two experiences.

Here, though, the surprise was even deeper.

The impact with the slums and the shacks, the misery and the rough lives of the women—with Rose's world, in short—did not just put me in front of a humanity that clenches the heart and a need whose extent I would not have understood from afar. It also made me see what allows Rose to face the full extent of this need, to affirm the full extent of this wounded humanity.

This book speaks of women rescued from poverty, from violence, from a sickness like AIDS, and from the marginalization that they live among their own people. It speaks about young people who, in those same conditions, have found a path to study and to cut out for themselves a future that would never have been theirs. It describes works—like the schools—that are amazing for their effectiveness and beauty. It shows what happens when NGOs work for the development of people and not for projects. But, when all is said and done, it documents one thing above all: the power that is unleashed by a human being when she discovers that her life has a value. It is greater than sickness or poverty. And it matters more than her limits.

The story of Rose, deep down, made me see this above all. And it did that through facts, faces, stories—sometimes so disconcerting as to be beyond measure. Yet real. So real that they pushed me to find myself in the words that she herself said, speaking about one of "her" women: "You look at her and say: 'How is it possible that she is happy? They have tortured and raped her, forced her to harm others, to eat human flesh.... How is she still standing?' But if she is still standing, why not me?"

So, at the end of the day: "how is it possible for her to be happy," even in these conditions? And if one who has lived through those things is still standing, "why not me?"

I think that these are questions that, in some way or another, touch all of us. I have certainly felt them—I feel them—as mine.

By a strange circumstance of destiny, I finished the first draft of this book the night before a stay in the hospital. It was not a particularly complex procedure but one of those that still leave you a little unsettled. I found myself thinking often of Rose there and of a phrase that I heard her say: "This morning I forgot about God. But He did not forget about me. I breathe."

In the end, her strength, which allows her and her women in Kampala to stand and sustain all that is living around them, comes from there: from this way of looking at themselves.

And I thought about this while I listened to my own breath and counted the beats of my heart: one, then another, and another still.... It was there. It might not have been there, but it was there.

Normally, nothing is more taken for granted. So often we live in an automatic, distracted way. Unaware.

But when you recognize it, something springs up that is capable of illuminating everything. And it makes everything fuller, more intense. As happens in Rose's world.

1

Kireka

THE SMELL. It is the first thing you notice when you step out of the car onto the strip of asphalt that runs along the hill. A bitter smell, sweat and iron-red earth and a whiff of carbon exhaust, relieved at times by the breeze that in these parts changes the sky so quickly. Now it is crystal clear. There is an intense mid-morning light, which cuts sideways through the alleys that here and there cut through the heart of the slum.

All around, wooden shacks and walls of stone and lime jut up against unpaved streets that are cut to make the water run down like streams when it rains hard. Every other house has a coat of light plaster. Here and there, there is some finished well, next to others where the roof is a metal sheet and some of the wood in the walls has pulled away, where you can see the smiling faces of children. Some goats, a strangely fat cat. And life, everywhere. Men on foot and on motorcycles. Many young people. But dominating everything, now, are the voices of women.

It is a surreal parade, down the small streets of Kireka. Laughter, hints of dancing, and greetings to those who come out to look from a stand with a handwritten sign that says "Restaurant" or from the slanted windows of their houses. There are a group of thirty women, with more joining them, who are making their way down the street. All different ages and all in different colored dresses. They walk. They sing. In front of a low house, with the owner seated in a tiny opening, they improvise a rhythmic song that draws out other smiling faces. You understand only "Corona," and from their gestures you intuit that they are telling the virus to leave and leave them in peace. And they dance, following the music that comes from a huge radio, one of those you find in Latino neighborhoods in the U.S.

Some carry a baby hanging on their back, wrapped in a woven cloth. Another has a baby in her arms. An old woman who comes across them exchanges a few words and breaks out into her own unique smile, with three teeth in her mouth but two eyes that shine out. There are a few masks about, more than you would expect, to remind you that the epidemic still threatens. All around there is the misery of the slum, one of the poorest neighborhoods in a poor capital like Kampala. But these women who are coming out of this shantytown, up toward the top of the hill, show something else.

They are from here: it is their home, and you see it after three steps. And yet they seem to have arrived from another world. You look at them; you speak about it. You are there together for hours, the whole walk, and before and after. But when you skim the adjectives one at a time, there is only one that seems adapted to what you see in front of you: "happy." A group of *happy* women. And among them, with eyes that are even more brilliant, there is a short little woman, with a green baseball cap and a white t-shirt, who is in the middle—not in front of—the group. Her skin is a little lighter than the others; some even joke and call her *muzungu*, white girl. She laughs and walks and dances with them. Happy indeed.

These are the same women that break rocks up above, in the quarry nestled in the hill and surrounded by shacks. They do it with long, thin hammers, little clubs with a wooden handle and a dark metal head: they strike once, a hundred, a thousand times, and the rocks become little pebbles and fine gravel, to be used in construction. 30 kilos, 100 shillings. A quarter of a dollar. They are there up to ten hours a day, with their backs covered by the bright colors bent under the sun, to carry home the equivalent of a few dollars. But many of them do it singing, as you see.

Just like you see them joking around two large metal trashcans from which emerge two thin tubes that lead to a basin of chipped metal, filled with rags and steam. It is their distillery: they boil millet and cassava with cane sugar and produce *waragi*, their type of gin. To drink or to sell in some of the shacks on the street. Or to offer to guests in a bottle that one of them, after a quick look at the one with the green cap, takes out of the bag: "Here, try it!"

You met others the day before, at Naguru. A similar neighborhood, with the same panorama: it seems even poorer, with the earth less red and less fertile. But those thirty women gathered under a canopy, in lines of five in front of a radio, are doing aerobics. Forty good minutes, without interruption. Following the steps of a young instructor, a woman was moving next to him and looking at him to replicate his motions. Sometimes with a certain elegance, other times out of sync. But she was laughing, happy. She danced. She sweated. And she kept on: twenty minutes, thirty, thirty-five . . . without stopping. And the others with her.

Behind the front row, they chased each other, tickled each other. There were secret slaps from one, while the other was trying to stretch. Someone played at fighting or pretending to put up her hands to defend herself, like a boxer. They seemed like children. And the one in the first row, that same green hat as today and the same scarf, was the most childlike of them all.

It is unsettling. Under that canopy, a little before, some of them had told you their stories. More than half are sick: HIV or even AIDS, not Covid. Almost all come from far away, from the North. Many escaped from the guerilla war years ago, sometimes carrying with them tremendous wounds that are still fresh: kidnapped by rebels, raped, forced to live for months in the bush, in the forest. Obligated to kill in order not to be killed, to steal children in hopes of one day returning to see theirs. Rejected by their own family or repudiated by their husbands. And yet they welcome the guest with songs and dances, and while they dance, they repeat a simple refrain: "Now I'm free."

How is this possible? And above all, who are they?

The trip to Uganda started from this question. Some of those women, in August 2021, were at the Meeting of Rimini, one of the biggest cultural events in Europe: six days of meetings, performances, exhibits, 150 speakers, and thousands of visitors, gathered under the umbrella of a title that serves as a common thread. In that case, the theme was "The courage to say 'I.'" And the women from Kampala were the center of an exhibit that told the story of their difficult world: "You are of value."

The contrast was quite striking there, in the first videos and in their terrible stories. But to see it here, in person, is a punch in the stomach. You understand even more the strength of that question which accompanied the photos and the stories: "And who am I?" There were phrases like this: "I had no hope, and I hated myself and my children"; "My husband abandoned me after he first infected me with HIV"; "No one wanted to be with me"; "I felt like a bag full of garbage." Dazed by the violence, the sickness, the wounds. . . . But they were alive, incredibly alive. And with that burning question: *Who am I?*

The subtitle of that exhibit was "Rose's Women." And Rose Busingye, fifty-four years old, a nurse, head of Meeting Point International in Kampala, is now there, among them, with her green hat that shadows her shy smile and a gaze that pierces you.

At first sight, while she dances in the middle of the group, she does not seem like a leader, the leader of the pack. It would not cross your mind, so to say, that here in front of you was a woman who has spoken at conferences and meetings all over the world. Who was called to the Vatican to present an encyclical and spoke many times to the pope and to the cardinals and bishops. Who received a prize from the most powerful women's association in America and the keys to the city of Florence. Who was the subject of a study by expert sociologists of development, and the protagonist of a documentary that received an award from Spike Lee at Cannes in 2008 and at the New York AIDS Film Festival the year before (it is called *Greater* and was filmed by a young director from Bologna, Emmanuel Exitu).

She is there, with her women and their wounds. She has accompanied them for thirty years on a journey that must have something extraordinary inside it. Otherwise, she would not have been able to carry a news story like the one that appeared on June 1, 2022 in the *L'Osservatore Romano*, the newspaper of the Vatican, with a drab title ("Solidarity without limits") but with surprising content: a story about them, the women of Meeting Point International, who had set aside some of their earnings from the quarry to make a donation to those who were suffering in Ukraine. A thousand Euros, enclosed in an envelope and handed over to the apostolic nuncio: "These are our tears asking God to take care of the Ukrainian people. Those people belong to us; they are in our heart."

It was not the first time, as we will see. But it is striking. Moreover, it is moving. And it makes the desire to understand even more acute: Who are these women? And who is Rose?

2

The Point of Departure

"YOU KNOW, here in Africa we talk a lot about development: but if one does not know he is of value, development does not exist." The white Toyota is descending slowly down the hill of Mbuya before turning left on New Port Bell Road and bending toward Kitintale, southwest of Kampala, while Rose says for the first time words that you will see become a reality in many ways in these days. "Development is the discovery of who you are and who the other is. Without this, you can do a thousand projects, but in the end they will be useless."

Rose has a round face that exudes joy. Large cheek bones, dark skin but not dark black, like the Acholi and the other Ugandans from the North, a small nose and pure eyes. Her gaze is sweet and deep at the same time: it reaches inside and reads you well. She laughs often: she makes fun of others and herself. Her voice is a light and slightly syncopated lullaby, like almost everyone here: it is part of the music of Africa. She speaks Italian very well, including the bad words—even if she says few of them and stops herself before finishing them, with a kind of modesty. In the following days, we will hear her sing in the Friulian dialect and even tell a joke with a few Neapolitan words thrown in.

Meanwhile, she says those words about development, and you think again about a video you saw on YouTube, just before leaving. It was a TV interview, where they asked her: "Who is the poor person?" And she said: "I think the poor person is the one who does not know the value of life. You can have everything and be desperate. Or you can find someone begging on the street and, instead of being desperate, he is happy. Because he has a reason for living."

Who knows how they will make those words apply to the reality that flows outside the car window. Kampala is a large city. It is hard to speak about a city center; the classic buildings of the financial district and the few towers (there are only eight of them over fifteen floors; the tallest is the Hilton with twenty-four floors and a height of just ninety meters) are spread out here and there. For someone coming for the first time, it is difficult to find points of reference. It takes a while to understand that the unity of measure, here, is not in the spaces, lines, and geometry that we are used to. It is the life, the human.

Men and women are everywhere. They are almost always young. Compared to Old Europe, it is another world: the median age—with half the population below—is 16 1/2 years of age (in Italy it is 46.2). They walk on the edge of the streets, beyond the ditches dug along the broken asphalt where, between the open holes on the red earth, there run cars, vans, and swarms of boda-boda—motor-taxis capable of carrying a whole family. Offices, shops, stalls are lined up one after the other. Women are sitting down selling fruit even at the edge of the train tracks. "They know when the train is passing by, and they get up all at once," explains Rose. There is a lot of green around. Red-tiled roofs, dark tanks for the rainwater. Occasionally, a few bigger houses, offices, a mall. But it is not enough to cover the view, which remains broad: from the street, you can almost always see the surrounding hills. Legend has it that there are seven, like Rome. In fact, you struggle to count them, but each certainly has its slum. And Meeting Point International,[4] which houses the offices of Rose and her staff, is on Mutungo Hill. A half turn on the circular road, then you enter on the right and stop suddenly in front of a wall and a gate. Two honks of the horn and the guard, slowly opens up. There is always a guard, twenty-four hours a day; but it is like this in all the residences in the city.

Rose's work starts from here, every morning. "At times, I stop by the Welcoming House first, especially if there is a problem. It is the house of welcome for the littlest ones. Then I come here. I meet those who need to speak to me; I see what needs to be done with the administration, the social work. And then I go into the field, the two Meeting Points that we have in the area." Each neighborhood, two visits a week: "Monday and Wednesday I am at Naguru; Tuesday and Thursday at Kireka: the majority of the work we do there." This would be the standard. But the only true rule, here, is the unforeseen.

In the meantime, the day has already started. Meeting Point is a small U-shaped building with an interior court covered by a blue plexiglass roof and divided by a large staircase. Just six steps and to the left is Rose's office. The floor is gritty; the white walls are spaced with doors and windows. The three sides of the building hold the offices, outside of which are benches and seats where those who arrive wait their turn. The other rooms are for the employees and social workers. Many are young and often children of the women of Kireka and Naguru. But also, some of the women work here. "The staff is made up of thirty-one people plus a few volunteers who maintain and clean the two Meeting Points in the slums," says Alberto Repossi, the only foreign face.

He is from Milan, forty-five years old, tall and thin with a short beard of five or six days. Repossi works for AVSI, the Italian NGO that helps Rose and her world:[5] he is her right-hand man in the office. "I take care of the operational aspects, the contracts. I try to do it so that she doesn't have to worry and can focus on educational questions." He gives a first sketch of the context. Between the Meeting Points in the two slums and the people who work here, there are more than 5,000 people who are helped: they receive healthcare, nutrition, education, English courses, the basics of domestic economy and microbusiness. Close to 2,000 of them have HIV. Two beautiful schools grew up around these people, one with more than 500 students, as well as an institute for forming teachers and a house to welcome abandoned babies. And a network of aid sustains 1,459 children from a distance.

But it is not the number that makes an impression. It is the life: the people that wait to meet Rose outside the office and the stories that come out from the social workers at their meeting. Fifteen of them, around a table where they meet each week. The meeting opens with a tally of those infected by Covid in the two slums. More than three hundred tests a week, a few positives: but the discussion is about how to convince parents not to bring their kids who have symptoms to school. Here there is a different atmosphere compared to the meetings we have: quiet voices, submissive tones. Maybe it is the presence of a foreigner, or maybe it is always like this. A couple of women, more advanced in age, have prepared a text and read the report they have prepared. At the end of every contribution, all the others thank them. You will understand later what path has led, over the years, to these women reading these pages here. The verb that you hear most is "share." The noun, "companionship." They discuss organizing a dance competition between Naguru and Kireka. "It would be a way to welcome new women and make them feel at home," says one of the social workers.

In the last few months, many new women have arrived. The social workers, or Rose herself, have gone out to find the families that need help. Or—as often happens—the women themselves have found the families. "If they find someone who has a problem, it is easy to say to them: 'Okay, Thursday, come to Meeting Point, there is a gathering,'" comments Repossi. They begin from there, from a life: games, songs, dances. Then they come to understand the problems, to collect information, to compile a record. And if there are children who need help, they can start the path that leads to financial sponsorship.

The workers regularly go to the slums: they visit families, they see houses, they determine if there are sick people or problems with school. They come up with reports, which they discuss together in their weekly meetings or evaluate right away, if it is something urgent. "One or two of them will always participate in Rose's meetings with the women," Repossi goes on to say. "It is there that Rose *shows her method*: which is not only to give advice, but to share an experience of life. Then, according to the needs, there can be a meeting on how to wash up well or how to cook the meat so that it doesn't lose its substance. But they are not default programs: they come out of reality."

It is the first pivotal point of a way of doing things that is revealed little by little: experience. To start from what happens, always, not from what is in the mind. "Rose reminds the social workers of this continuously: 'Do not preach, do not give advice. Listen. You have to help the person understand what she is living, in such a way that she herself can imagine the solution. She has to understand the steps she has to take.' The social worker is not there to solve problems, but to help the other grow."

This does not happen often in the world of development. It is easier for one to arrive on the scene with a model already on hand and recipes to apply. Except that then you find yourself in trouble when reality presents itself as more complicated than you foresaw, or when it changes all of a sudden. Just as it did with Covid. The first stories that surprise you come from the Covid emergency; they are a chronicle of the pandemic.

"The virus brought not only contagion but also hunger," Repossi explains. "It is very much a hand-to-mouth economy: you eat if you earn something that day." If the markets are closed, the stalls on the street are forbidden, and the people are not out and about, that evening you put nothing on the table. The government provided some food distribution, a one-time thing.

From Meeting Point, also thanks to international help, there were sacks of flour, oil, salt, sugar that the families took from these offices.

Many lost their houses along with their jobs. "Here almost everyone rents; they have land or a house in the villages, to the North," Repossi continues. Those who could not go to the market to sell, and so to pay their rent, sometimes found themselves thrown outside from evening to morning. "But in the slums, we saw women who welcomed their friends or their children," in houses that are often shacks, usually a couple of rooms separated by a sheet. "You saw these families confined to ten or twelve square meters with someone sleeping out on the porch.... It was a great lesson for us."

It is a solidarity bigger than the earlier Covid emergency, and it has deep roots. Repossi speaks about a family "with three daughters that welcomed four children who had been abandoned on the street." Or about a mother "who died and left two children. The smallest one was very malnourished, and we brought him to Welcoming House. Rose asked if there was someone who could welcome the older brother, and a family took him to live with them."

A few years ago, Odida, one of the women from the slum, was asked if she could host an abandoned little girl at her house. "She did it. And it was crazy, because if you see her now, she who is not the natural child is the same for the adoptive mother. The same!" Last year Odida had a stroke and was semi-paralyzed. And now it is that little girl who helps her the most: she gives a hand with the cleaning, helps her walk. "But there are so many stories like this. And they make me see a humanity that flourishes where you never expected it," says Repossi. "Here it is unthinkable for a family to welcome the child of another, above all if he or she is not from the same tribe."

Unthinkable, and yet it happens. Why? And what does this have to do with the comings and goings that you see around Rose's office, across from Repossi's office? The offices are about eight square meters, with desks full of papers, a fan, a photo of Father Giussani—the priest from Brianza who founded Communion and Liberation—and who was born just over a hundred years ago, in 1922. There are flyers and a T-shirt with the Meeting Point logo: it is a reproduction of a painting by Eugène Burnand, the Swiss painter—Peter and John running to the tomb, after the Resurrection of Christ. Hundreds of lives and problems pass through this little room. What is the difference in the way Rose faces these lives and helps them?

"Come, now it is time to go to Kireka." Rose gets back into the white Toyota; the gate opens again. After the first turns, she responds: "How did all this begin? Deep down, there is only one point of departure: God was moved toward me, who was nothing. Who *am* nothing."

And she begins to tell her story.

3

The Encounter

"THE PEARL OF AFRICA." It is difficult to open a book about Uganda without finding this characterization. But it is right on the money: when the English explorer Henry Stanley first set foot here, in 1875, it came naturally to him to use this phrase. It was green, it had water, fertile soil, a temperate climate that seldom reached 85°F. It was also rich in natural resources, but this would only come to be understood later. What was immediately clear instead was that the region was already a mix of languages and tribes. In what was then called the Kingdom of Buganda, 240,000 square kilometers near the source of the Nile River and facing Lake Victoria (1 1/2 times larger than the Po Valley in Italy), there were more than fifty ethnic groups. An English protectorate since 1894, independent since 1962, riven by civil and tribal wars before and after, the country through which the Equator crosses has always maintained two characteristics: a land that is good and, all things considered, open.

Even today, Uganda is rated third in the world in hospitality: it hosts almost 1.5 million refugees, according to UNHCR data. Many have arrived over time due to tragedies in neighboring countries: South Sudan, Burundi, the Congo.... They live in settlements that resemble the classic refugee camps spread across Africa: they are more than villages, with markets and services and sometimes little vegetable gardens assigned to those who arrive there. These settlements are located above all in the West Nile, where 55 percent of the refugees have found a place; in districts like Adjumani and Moyo, refugees make up over half the local population.

"You know, in the end, compared to other countries, we are doing well here," says Rose. "Certainly, there are divisions: every tribe has its language. It is a little like the Tower of Babel: to talk among ourselves we need to learn English. And if you ask, 'but which are the Ugandan people?' I don't know if you can find out. Everyone came from outside. But if you don't cause problems, no one looks to see if you are an immigrant or not."

Neither is Rose Ugandan. At least, not originally. Her family arrived from the South, from Rwanda, during the 1960s. They are Tutsi and also have some ancestry from the ancient royal line: a distant connection, but not enough to shelter the family from harm when the country, after independence in 1962, was ravaged by civil wars and massacres. The Busingyes crossed the border and settled in Kabale, a town of 40,000 inhabitants. "We were neither rich nor poor. Dad had cows, mom taught for a few years, then, with the arrival of children, she left her job." After a little while, they also had to abandon Kabale: it was too close to Rwanda to be secure. Their new house was in Kampala, the capital.

Frederick Busingye was "a calm man. He did not talk a lot, but he made himself understood: when he said 'enough,' it was 'enough.' My mom was more chatty." Her name was Susanna, her daughter looks a lot like her. She was "short, sunny, always smiling, the same luminous eyes, the same cheekbones that stick out a bit," recalls Clara Broggi, a former teacher and international collaborator, one of the first friends Rose would meet in Italy. Above all, she had a sharp, deep faith. "When she left the house, she made the sign of the cross: 'You who make me go out, let me come back,'" recalls Broggi. "She thanked God for everything. But she was not self-righteous: faith was a part of her, her way of being."

Rose was born in 1968, into a family that already had three children. "They waited for me for almost ten years; I arrived when they thought that they wouldn't have any more children." Instead she was added to the two older brothers, Francis Xavier and Emanuel, and to her sister Goretti. Very Catholic names, because the imprint of the family is clear. Rose has an uncle, Francis, who is a priest; another became a bishop.

"I was born a Catholic Christian," she says. "My mother baptized me right away: she could not wait even a day for her child to be baptized. But growing up, those words—Jesus, faith, prayer—didn't mean anything important to me. I saw my mother who sat at the table praying, she pulled a potato out of the garden and made the sign of the cross.... It seemed a little exaggerated to me. In the evening, she prayed the rosary with my siblings. I couldn't do it; I fell asleep before it was over. In short, I never thought that God did not exist, but it wasn't something for me. I was convinced that God needed pure people, capable people like my mother. I thought that I was not worthy. And it was like this until I met Father Tiboni."

Pietro Tiboni was a Comboni missionary.[6] Born in 1925, from Tiarno near Trent—a few kilometers from Lake Garda, the land of Saint Daniele Comboni, the founder of his order—he graduated in Philosophy and Theology, already a brilliant student of Father Cornelio Fabro (one of the greatest Italian philosophers of the twentieth century). At the crossroads between an academic career and the missions, he didn't have a doubt: "My Rome is Africa." He arrived in South Sudan in 1957. He came back to Italy seven years later when the government expelled many of the missionaries from Sudan. And in 1970, he received a new destination: Kitgum, northern Uganda, where he was parish priest and, a little later, founded a seminary for older vocations, the Pastoral Institute of Kitgum.

It was there that Tiboni encountered a small group of young Italians who made him curious and then attracted him. They were mostly doctors, a few teachers, almost all from the area around the city of Varese, just north of Milan. Arriving with their families in 1969, they worked in the hospitals and missions of the area between Kitgum and Gulu. And they were from Communion and Liberation, one of the first groups of people from the movement who left to bring the charism of Father Giussani out into the world.

Tiboni was struck by their way of living, by the "fact that they put Christ at the center of everything," in the words of Father Giussani himself, whose texts he began to read. And when the founder of CL came to Kitgum in 1971 to visit, Tiboni went to meet him. The harmony between the two was immediate. Speaking about those days, years later, the Comboni missionary would say: "I do not remember a word of our encounter: but the impression that he made on me was something exceptional."

Tiboni got involved with CL. He strengthened those connections when another typically African crisis brought him to Rome. In 1975, the regime of Idi Amin Dada, in retaliation against a bishop who was opposed to the government, expelled him together with fourteen of his confreres. He had entered emphatically into responsibility for the movement locally when the political situation in Uganda allowed him to return in 1980. In August 1981, with a group of friends during the National Theological Week, he offered to the Ugandan Church what remains known as "the Katigondo proposal," from the name of the locality where he carried out his work: he launched the Christ Communion and Life movement. The initials have an extra "C" and the name is different because the word "Liberation" would have made the government suspicious, but the substance is there: it is CL in Uganda.

A few years later, in a testimony at the Rimini Meeting, Tiboni would summarize it like this: "Our work was based on two very simple points: 1) the discovery of an infinite desire in ourselves; 2) the discovery that Jesus Christ is the answer to this desire.... The judgment that the Africans were different than the Europeans was widespread, or than the Americans or than others, and, in fact, between people of a different culture that live in different situations there is an enormous difference.... But when we ask the fundamental question, when we help people to ask themselves 'Who am I?'—when we help them to discover that desire for truth and happiness that we find in ourselves—then the people wake as from a dream and find themselves perfectly united and equal and there is no difference between African and Chinese.... In front of the fundamental questions there is no longer any difference between people as long as they look at each other from this point of view, as men and women created by God whose destiny is Jesus Christ. When instead we lack this perspective, it is clear that the differences and divisions are infinite...."

Rose met Father Tiboni when she was still practically a child, in the church that is still her parish today: Our Lady of Africa. It is a large twelve-sided building made of cement and wood, with the Stations of the Cross in glass. Long pews. At the entrance to the small parking lot is a huge crucifix. "I was coming to Mass here. I grew up in this neighborhood; we participated a little in the oratory; they organized gatherings for young people. And one time, Father Tiboni, who lived in the Comboni house near here, came. We chatted, he gave me a little picture, something to read." Rose was twelve years old. "I had not understood that Tiboni was speaking to me about CCL: but what he was talking about was a God so strange that I wanted to understand. He had become something interesting for me. I wanted to know more."

Rose spoke about her encounter with Tiboni at her first Rimini Meeting in 1991.[7] "The first proposal of the movement I had was through him. I was struck by one of his phrases: 'The Church has to be a movement; many people risk their lives because of politics or defending their houses, but no one does all this for Christ and for the salvation of the nation.'" Rose added that she had made a second discovery "determinative for me: prayer." The reason? "What is impossible for man is possible for God. Often we are tempted to do things according to our projects or on the basis of our capacity and strength; but through prayer I learned to ask Christ to enter always, to be present in every aspect of life. As I learned from Father Tiboni, to begin anything without prayer is like starting a game with a broken leg."

There is a book that tells the story of the beginnings of CL in Uganda, titled *La difficile speranza* [*The Difficult Hope*], which came out in 1986 and was written by Enrico Castelli, a journalist from Varese who would become a known face on Italian television.[8]

Of value in helping orient us in the troubling events of the seventies and eighties, with the coming and going of coups d'etat and strong men (from Milton Obote to Idi Amin Dada, then again Obote and finally Yoweri Museveni, who came to power in 1986 and is still in charge), the volume is also striking for various reasons.

First of all, the stature of Father Tiboni. Possessed of a fine mind and a large humanity, he always perceived that for a missionary it could never be enough to "do": the needs are infinite, but organizational activism is not the key to having a *true* impact on Africa's problems. The encounter with Giussani, this strange intertwining of charisms—CL and the Comboni missionaries—made him grasp the challenge in greater depth.

In a first little book of "directives on the Christian method," addressed first to young people and to his Comboni brothers who were getting close to the movement, he wrote:

> When we propose Christ Communion and Life to someone, right away they ask us a few fundamental questions. The first is: "What should we do?" It is important to continue to look for the presence of Jesus Christ. This will change life. The other questions are: "What are the aims and goals of CCL? The other associations have a program and a method: what is yours?" In effect, many movements have the aim of renewing the Church and society. CCL follows a completely different line. We can even say that it follows an inverse procedure. The point of departure is the subject—that is, the person—not a goal to be reached. It is two or three people who have the intuition that Christ is important for them get together to deepen their faith and their communion. This work will change their mentality and their attitude toward people and things.

It is a proposal that goes deeper than so many organizational attempts and pastoral plans for evangelization. And it intersects well with the needs of a historical moment in which, as the Ugandan Episcopal Conference wrote in a document, "we live in a country where everything is expensive and only human life is cheap." The conclusion of the bishops: "We must re-form consciences: there cannot be justice without the renewal of the person." The idea of the Comboni priest goes exactly in that direction.

But Tiboni is also a pastor, not only a theologian: he knows how to accompany people, to help them grow. In Castelli's book, we find dozens of dialogues and exchanges of letters that confirm this. And they evoke another powerful aspect of the CCL experience: the radicality with which the first Ugandan youth engaged and lived it.

There are amazing testimonies. To begin with the testimony of Francis Bakanibona, just twenty years old, whom Father Giussani would call "our first martyr": he was a catechist in Kasala, a village to the north of Kampala, and was killed on 22 November 1982, beaten and stabbed by militants of the Obote government, who accused him—wrongly—of helping Museveni's rebels. He died outside the church, saying: "Lord, forgive them. I am dying for no reason. I know nothing. Forgive them. Jesus was treated in the same way." He had met the movement three months earlier. And he had just written a letter to a Comboni missionary, a friend of Tiboni, in which he told how his life had changed: "People say: 'You are totally different from others, both in how you speak and how you comport yourselves.' And in this way, those who discover our way of life are united to us and are happy when we tell them about CCL.... Pray for us and for our people, so that we may understand that only through Christ can we have peace and freedom."

Other facts are striking, especially if we consider that the protagonists were adolescents or a little older. There is Judith, a young mother of two children born out of wedlock, who after meeting CCL brings peace to her family of origin, where one brother had accused another of being a guerrilla and had him arrested. There is Andrew, detained in Luzira, the jail where political prisoners are kept (and where a Comboni missionary from the movement helps as chaplain), who in a letter tells about his quarrel with Ben, "tall and big in a scary way" and of an embrace that would have been impossible "if Father Gregorio had not spoken to us about the forgiveness of Christ and of the gesture of the pope [he was speaking about John Paul II who had forgiven Ali Agca, his assassin]." There is Simon, supervisor at a textile business, who writes of how a colleague had offered him shillings "for your secret medicine, because I see that here, with you, people work better, they are happy, and I want to know what you are giving them." There are testimonies of young students, Geoffrey, Betty, Caroline, protagonists of simple episodes that would never end up in the newspapers but show a seed of newness. "When I meet them or they come to Kampala, I find them happy," Tiboni will write. "Why are they doing well? Because the unity among them, without distinction of color, is so great and intense that it is as if there was only one face."

One of those young people was Rose. At the time, she was fourteen years old. "I wrote often to Tiboni," she recalls now. "But every now and then he stole something from my diary." It was Tiboni himself who suggested that she write him, to reflect on her experience. And some pages, which ended up in Castelli's book, are impressive for their maturity, first for that subtle game between life and death that looms over every instant of the day, even the most normal.

"While we were returning from school, a soldier stopped me and a friend, pushing his rifle against us," writes Rose in a letter from December 1982.

> When I felt that rifle on my cheek, I dropped my gaze and started to recite the Consecration to Mary to myself.[9] The soldier said: "I am going to kill you," and soon after he took away our bags. He wanted our socks and shoes. Then he told us to go and tell everything to the police, but while we were walking away, I saw that he was opening fire on us. The moment he started shooting, though, something didn't work. The rifle fell to the ground. The two of us began to run, all the way home. I told my friend: "Did you see what the Lord did for us? Through the Virgin, he spared our lives. Let's go pray for the soldier. Even if he took our things, he is still our brother, and I want his good." The girl said to me: "You are different. No one can understand you."

This difference is already noticeable in Rose. It is not a question of character: she does not have the spirit of a leader, and, as some who knew her at that time say, she was "very shy," an aspect that will remain with her. No, there is another origin: it is the beginning of her belonging to something *other*.

"The students, when they come to school, are good: but after a little bit, they change: they do not study, and they want to go into the city," she writes in a page of her diary.

> If you do not go with them, they begin to hate you. Any good word you say, they do not listen, unless you indicate to the girls how to get money and to the guys where to find girls. I don't have any way to get money. Every day I put on the same dress, I don't have a watch or anything beautiful that girls cannot get except from

lovers. One of them said to me: "Why don't you get a boyfriend who can get you everything you want?" I answered her: "No one can love me more than God and God who created me has an inseparable love for me, more than any other, even more than my father and mother." And she: "Why then do you not ask Him for dresses and other things?" I answered her: "He gives me things that are necessary. You can have many things of this world but lose eternal life. And then what advantage is there in having many things and losing your life?" ... When they see our group at school many people ask us what tribe we belong to and where we come from. And when they see that we help each other they are confused, because we do it even if we are not from the same tribe.

Some of these writings were already circulating in Italy before Castelli's book. In an article in *Litterae Communionis*, the monthly magazine of CL, the cover of the February 1983 issue was dedicated to "Rose's Diary." In the abstract of the article we read: "A young Ugandan student recounts day by day the discovery of Christ and the proposal of the community as the only possibility of peace among the hatreds and divisions that tear the African country." In the text, after a brief introduction and alongside many episodes of daily life similar to those we have already recounted, there are reflections like this: "I cried like a baby without her mother. One time I felt myself so alone that my thought was on the emptiness and I asked myself: 'Why can't God save me from this solitude and give me someone who can nourish me with the word of salvation?'" Or again: "I have to look for a friend who can participate in the gift that brings peace and joy to life. I feel that my friends should follow me and thus have the possibility of reconciling their heart; all my friends, without excluding those that are my enemies." And again: "After I encountered it, the movement has taken my whole heart. I feel that God wants something from me. God has sent his disciple to teach me his word."

But the most moving fact is recounted in a letter sent to an Italian friend in 1984, reproduced in Castelli's book:

> For the vacation I went home because they wrote to me that my sister had been killed by her husband. He wanted to marry a Protestant girl and everyone said that Catholics are guerillas. So they killed my sister at home: they cut her with a hoe. When I heard this, I was shocked. My heart was full of fear; but I prayed with authority through Mary to be able to overcome and conquer all this. When I arrived home, I found everyone full of fear and hatred. I prayed for them: when I entered, some of them were thinking

about revenge. I asked my mother: "Why do you not begin to love, right away? God exists, God loves us. We have to communicate this love to others. He gave his son for us. We have to begin now, together, because no one loves or prays for those they hate. God is the one who brings justice, you have to forgive and pray. God gives and God takes. All that happens is his. It is the will of God, it must be carried out." Immediately my mother got down on her knees. She asked forgiveness from God for what she had thought and was always happy during the rest of my stay. I find that trusting prayer through Mary has helped me, because even I am full of fear and do not know what I can say to them. The people were strange, full of hatred and they found that instead I had a heart full of forgiveness. I also invited them to unite themselves to my prayer for that man who had killed my sister, so that he could change and repent of what he had done. The others thought that I was acting and did not believe me: only my mother took me seriously. She told me: "I want you to continue to believe in this faith, so that you can come and remind me of what I should do, because these are not just your words but a message from God, that has made me feel new, like I was coming out of a nightmare. Continue. I will pray for you and your friends that help you in this. Tell them to pray for me, because I am a sinful woman."

Father Giussani read the same letter some months later in a meeting with students from Bocconi University in Milan, "as an example of the most divine thing that Christ has brought to earth, a letter that I intend to read everywhere. It is another world! It is another world lived in this world."[10]

When you ask her about that letter and about her sister, Rose looks into the distance. "It is true. It happened like that."

We understand why the friendship with "Tibo," as everyone called him, was decisive for her. "He was very different from the other priests," she says. "I was going to church, also because my mom pushed me. I had for a long time heard certain words. But when I asked questions, he took me seriously. He looked at me and answered calmly. I thought no one, not even my uncles who are priests, was like that. They were concerned that I be good: "obey, pray, and go to confession." To see this priest who took me to heart, as if I was a daughter for him, was different. I went to go see him willingly. I met the movement with him, and I lived it with him."

It is thanks to Tiboni that Rose came across a few pages of Father Giussani for the first time. And she found there a phrase that was imprinted within her: "The Mystery was made flesh." These are the same words that for the founder of CL marked what he called "the beautiful day," the foundational discovery of his life, which he made listening to a professor in the seminary: "The Word of God—that is, that of which everything is made—was made flesh. Therefore beauty was made flesh, goodness was made flesh, justice was made flesh, love, life, truth were made flesh: being is not in some Platonic realm, it was made flesh, it is one of us."[11]

"I had read the Bible; I had heard those words many times," says Rose. "Many others had told me that God became flesh. But not in that way. The way Father Giussani said it struck me. It was something strange. New. I went to Tiboni and asked him: 'Does this flesh that he talks about here have something to do with *my* flesh?'" And while she speaks, with her face just as if it were happening now, she pinches the back of her hand with two fingers, to underline that she is talking about her, about *her* being. Tiboni took her very seriously, even that day: "He looked at me and said: 'Yes, it has to do with your flesh. Because we are poor, wretched: and God came for me and for you. If we were great and capable, God would not have come to earth. Instead it is for you and for me that he came, because we are poor sinners.'"

Those words, in some way, signal a turnaround. "Meeting Giussani and discovering my vocation coincided. And I owe it to Tiboni, to how he embraced me."

The missionary had also understood for some time that there was something special in that girl. With the agreement of her family, he helps her to study. He sends her to the North, to Gulu, where there is a high school run by the Little Sisters of Mary Immaculate. "It was fine with my parents. For my mother, the fact that Tiboni was involved was essential. A priest for her was an authority: a kind of Melchizedek, the priest in the Bible anointed by the Lord. Let alone with Tibo, whom she knew so well. . . ." She laughs. And then, seriously: "That time was a grace for me."

Once again, through Tiboni, Rose has another experience that will have a huge effect on her life: a trip to Kitgum, to meet the families of the Italian doctors who live there. It was meant to last just a couple of days, but instead, right at that moment, the conflicts between the rebels of Tito Okello and the government of Museveni, who had just taken power, were inflamed. Many roads to the North were closed. The visit to the friends became a journey of weeks, then a few months.

"Rose remained at our house for a good while," recalls Samuele Rizzo, known by everyone as "Sasà," who today works for AVSI and is the son of Ivone, one of the first doctors who arrived as missionaries from Varese. "It was 1986, and Tiboni had asked us to host her. She had already thought about becoming a nurse, and my father took her around on his visits. Then, as soon as she saw blood, Rose would faint. Always. He was a surgeon, so you can imagine. . . ." She was eighteen years old; Samuele was a baby. "But I remember her well, at home: she was the shyest person I had ever met. At table, for example, she always remained silent." Samuele, though, remembers something else, which Tiboni shared some time later: "He was also struck by the shyness of Rose: he said that it was not only her character, but something more, something sacred. He called it 'the shyness of God.' It was at such a profound level, so much hers, that Tiboni said: 'Only God can understand her. It is like a prayer.' He was right: if you see her now, the shyness of Rose is very different. But it is still there."

In fact, when Rose returned to Kampala, her decision to become a nurse was solid. "I had seen many people suffer because of the war. Hospitals that did not work, people who died, wounded people who arrived and had no one to take care of them. They died, and it was like somebody's chicken had died. It was very painful for me. . . . When I returned here, I decided to do the course that they call 'medical assistant.'" It was a kind of high-level nursing school. She studied at Nsambya, one of the most important hospitals in Kampala.

During her studies, she came across another foundational text. It was an article in *30 Giorni* [*30 Days*], an international monthly magazine from the CL world: it covered topics in the Church, and in the eighties and nineties it became one of the most widespread and authoritative magazines in the area. That text, by Lucio Brunelli and Gianni Cardinale, is an interview with Father Giussani and speaks about the Memores Domini, "a new 'association' approved by the Holy See. Its aim: to live the memory of Christ in the world of work."[12] It begins like this: "They hold their goods in common, they practice chastity and live under obedience, but they do not wear religious habits or take vows. They dedicate at least two hours each day to prayer and contemplation, but they are 'entirely immersed in the world,' and they earn their living by their own work, like everyone else. It was not easy to find a place in the canon law of the Church for these lay monks of our time who call themselves *Memores Domini*—those who live the memory of the Lord."

In the dialogue, Father Giussani talks about the life and aims of what the people in CL call "Gruppo Adulto": the Church, a few months earlier, on December 8, 1988, recognized it as a "universal private ecclesial association," and it already included "several hundred members, both men and women (with a slight majority of the latter), and houses in Europe, Africa, and Latin America," wrote the two authors.

Rose read it and was blown away: "It was speaking about people who live the memory of Christ in every aspect of their life. I went to Tiboni and told him: who are these people? Why did you never tell me that something like this existed?" The missionary's answer made her even more curious: "Rose, they are adult men and women, responsible for their destiny. They have made a definitive choice." "And I thought: 'Responsible.... This is something huge. I am not responsible.' But instead it was like a fire had been lit, and it burned. Always more and more. After a little bit I went back to Tiboni: 'But can I go see Father Giussani and ask him about this thing?' And he: 'Yes, but be aware that you are very young: they are adults, grown-ups.... Finish your exams first, and then go. They live that memory about which they speak in their work.'"

"That dialogue gave me a true reason to study," continues Rose. "I set myself to study like I had never studied before. My fears disappeared, I saw the whole horizon. Many were telling me: 'But there is no Gruppo Adulto here.' But for me it was something that had already taken hold of me. It had become me, and no one could take me away from there. It would have been like tearing off my skin. When I went to my mom and told her: 'I am going to the Memores,' and I didn't even know very well what they were, she answered: 'Yes, go. If God wants you with Him, He will take you. If he doesn't want you, you will return to me.' I was afraid of leaving. I asked myself: 'Who are they, how do they live?' I had never seen a house of the Gruppo Adulto. But I went, saying: 'If God wants me, He will take me, if He does not want me, I will come back.'"

She took her exams and passed. "And I didn't even wait to collect my diploma: I left right away for Italy."

4

The Embrace

WHEN SHE ARRIVED in Italy on 20 June 1990, Rose met three women from the Memores Domini house in Varese there to welcome her. "There was the Fraternity of Uganda [a group formed to sustain friends from Varese on mission in the African country], certain other contacts: Father Giussani thought about sending her there because in some way there was already a connection," recalls Clara Broggi. She too was from Varese and would be among those closest to Rose, given that she would leave for Kampala within a few years.

That day in June 1990, though, she confesses that "we were a little intimidated, and not only because we were asking ourselves how we were going to understand each other: Rose was not famous like today, but in the movement she was spoken about; we had already read some of her things, even if we did not know what she looked like." They found themselves in front of a shy young girl:

> She gets off the plane and she didn't even know where to turn, where to pick up her things. "Are you Rose? Let's go to the house." Obviously none of us could speak properly to each other. But we made ourselves understood. At a certain point, the day after, she asks me: "On the road where we were driving yesterday, where do the people walk? And that lady inside the box, is she there the whole day?" The box was the toll booth on the freeway. Things like this, in short, that made you laugh. Above all at the beginning, she seemed to us like a porcelain doll. We tried not to tire her out, to be totally at her service.

Those texts in *Litterae Communionis* and the letter on forgiveness to her sister's killers—which Father Giussani also read at the Memores retreat—in some way created an expectation, a curiosity. "We watched her with reverence and a bit of trepidation at the same time. But I, for example, thought every now and then: 'It all seems a little exaggerated to me.' I had remained struck by that letter, and had said to myself: 'How did she come to forgive?' But it almost seemed excessive, far from our way of doing things."

Rose, for her part, found herself catapulted into another world. And if you ask her what ultimately brought her there, what she was looking for when she came across those words of Giussani, her answer is disarming: "Look, I don't know. It seemed to me that in that moment I was not looking for anything. It was like this. I knew that God was not for me, because I am full of sins. And what should I have looked for, if there was no room for me in the heart of God? I was there, like . . . ashamed. To find this phrase of John's Gospel, to hear that God had become flesh, was as if the possibility to enter into that heart where I thought there was no space had been given to me."

Even the first encounter with Father Giussani was not normal. Rose tells it like this:

> After a few weeks in Italy, they brought me to a vacation in Corvara [an annual meeting of the international leaders of CL that was then held in a place in the Val Badia]. I arrive at the hotel, they give me the key and I went toward the room. And I saw in the hall someone praying the rosary walking back and forth with a long, light green coat. In Uganda, we had at the most only a few copies of *Litterae Communionis*, I didn't know what Father Giussani looked like.

She gets to the elevator. She enters, and so does he:

> He looks at me from head to toe and says: "Are you Rose?" And I: "Are you Father Giussani?" He hugged me. I remained there, with the elevator that was opening and closing, and no one was able to press the button . . . . But it was an embrace like I had never experienced in my life. I attended that whole vacation without even hearing anything that was said: I only had in mind that gaze and that embrace.

The true and proper meeting, though, happened a few days later, in September. "They call me, I go there with Tiboni. And Giussani says to me: 'Look, the directors of the Memores are all in agreement that you should make your profession.'" It was a totally unusual occurrence. In the Gruppo Adulto, before making definitive promises, there is a course of verification and novitiate that normally lasts at least five years. It was clear that the talk with Father Tiboni had convinced everyone: there was a maturity in that young girl that was truly extraordinary.

"I had prepared so many speeches, so many questions," recalls Rose. "At home they had told me that it would take years, above all because I was so young. And he, instead, tells me this thing about the profession. 'But Father Giussani, do you know how old I am?' 'Don't worry, even if you were only five years old I would have done the same thing.' 'Are you sure? I have only read a magazine. I don't even know what the Memores are.' 'Do you love Jesus?' There, yes, I felt that I really knew what I was saying: 'Yes. Yes, I love him.' 'And do you want to give your life for him?' I told him: 'No.' Giussani was a bit shaken: 'Why not?' And I: 'Look, Father Gius, I don't know... I do not have anything important in my life to give to Jesus. I am nothing. But I want him to take also this nothingness that I feel.' He slapped the table, jumped up, and told me something that I have never forgotten: 'Tell that to everyone, always! Because everyone wants to give something important to Jesus and in this way, their whole life, it is like they expected something in return. And instead it is he who takes our nothing and saves it!'"

"I felt like I was in front of someone who saw inside me," says Rose. "And then you pour over everything that you feel: your nothingness, your sin.... At a certain point, he took my hand and said: 'Do you know, Rose, even if you were the only human being on the earth, God would have come all the same.' He stopped and then continued: 'He came for you. Because God does not come to earth for a group of men. In front of him, every person is unique. God came for you, for you He went to the cross, for you He died and rose. For the value that you have. And He will be with you every day, so that your nothingness may not be lost.'"

For her, they are fundamental words. "I don't know how to say it in another way, but I felt for the first time an attraction, a love for myself, as if I had never truly looked at myself before," she says. "I was overcome by a great tenderness, for myself and for everything. I wanted to shout to everyone that life has a meaning, that there is a significance in everything: even in sleeping, in suffering, in death. There is a meaning."

Clara Broggi was outside that door. "I had gone with her. When she came out, I thought I didn't understand. I asked Father Gius: 'Excuse me, what should the girl do?' And he, even a little annoyed: 'I already told you:

the profession, at the Advent retreat.'" Broggi says that she had only one thought: "That it was right. That is, in itself it was something incredible. But to me it seemed that it was right that she should do it. I have never seen anyone live the presence of Jesus with the normality with which she lives it. In everything. It is amazing."

Rose became a Memor Domini on December 1st that year. She lived in the house in Varese where she was being hosted. "There were twenty women with me," she recalls, before listing a series of names: "*The* Elena, *the* Franchina, *the* Clara." All with the article before, as it is used in Lombardy. "There was Franca, the head of the house, who became one of my best friends. Giovanna, with whom I joked around a lot. We had fun in that house."

So many of these companions, in time, would move to Kampala, at least for a while. But during those two years in Varese, Rose grew a lot. "Being with them helped me walk. I was like a child: they took care of me, they taught me how to speak, how to eat. They taught me everything. And in fact I really love that house, because it is my house. It is there that every day it seemed like I was going up a staircase: one step, then another. With all my failures, I gradually learned how to walk."

"In the beginning, she kind of made a mess," says Broggi. "She did not have much of an idea what it meant to be in a Gruppo Adulto house. I don't know, there was silence [the Memores Domini live some time of the day and of the week respecting silence] and she was listening to music and singing to herself. 'Rose, it's time for silence!' 'But I am not singing loudly. . . .' Things like this, in short. Simple things. Then, little by little she gained confidence, she began to make jokes, because she is really very kind, she likes to laugh: like the night procession dressed as ghosts. . . ."

Very normal things, like with a child. "Deep down, what strikes me the most about Rose is that she is a totally normal person: I have seen her in trouble so many times, I have seen her get upset over nothing, I have seen her react like I react. She is not a saint. Yet she is one in whom you really see the work of Jesus. You see this work a little bit in everybody, surely: but in her you see it writ large." Examples?

> I'm saying, she never seems to get jealous or envious. Things that are always there somewhat in us, in some way, they come out. No, she does not know what they are. It seems impossible but that's how it is. Even in the small things. I don't know: she went out somewhere and came back with a gift only for one of us. What

would we do? We would give it to that person in private, so as not to make the others upset. She wouldn't do it like that, not at all. She would give that thing in front of everyone, without even thinking that another could get offended, because she would not be offended. She is totally free from all these dynamics, even in the particulars. It is a characteristic that has always struck me a lot.

She has remained with this childlike heart. Maybe it has even grown over the years. It has gotten deeper, fuller. And this is the other thing that strikes you, being with her: you have the strong impression of an extreme simplicity and, together with that, a fullness.

"Whoever meets her, and sees what is born around her, notices a kind of disproportion," says Davide Prosperi, fifty years old, professor of Biochemistry at the University of Milan. He has been the president of the Fraternity of CL since November 2021, but for Rose he is "a precious friend" from before (they met each other in the mid-nineties, when he invited her to a meeting in his faculty). "You have in front of you an extremely humble person. And I speak of that real *humilitas*, of that connection with the earth: her faith is unshakeable and also very concrete—'earthy,' to be precise. But this humility is such that she is not afraid to be corrected, and to learn, even from people that would not be capable of doing what she has done. This really amazes me. Because it indicates that she knows that she belongs totally, without shadow, to something greater than herself: to Christ."

"She is transparent, in every sense," says Ignacio "Nacho" Carbajosa, a Spanish priest who became a great friend of Rose when he started going to Uganda to accompany Ugandan university students, "and this makes friendship more simple."

In those two years in Lombardy, Rose had a scholarship at the hospital in Varese. She specialized in infectious diseases but also studied obstetrics. And obviously, she worked in hospital wards. It was there that her vocation to work matured in a full way. She came face to face with a disease that was emerging with force in those years, AIDS. And she clung to friendships that would remain for her whole life, within and outside the movement.

Giorgio Vittadini—professor of statistics at the Bicocca University in Milan, president of the Foundation for Subsidiarity, and a CL leader since the 1980s—tells about a person he met in a roundabout way in those years, "whose name I won't mention for obvious reason: at that time, in short, he was a thief. He had a girlfriend who was sick with AIDS and recovering in

Varese. He had nothing to do with the faith and the Church, but going there to meet his partner, he saw this black nurse who embraced the sick people and was with them. He began to think: 'This is not possible. Here even the relatives keep their distance, because they are afraid of getting infected. How is she able to do this?' He met her. And there his path of conversion began. Then, when she went away, she introduced him to me." That man remained connected to Rose and to her story. "One of the orphan children from the Welcoming House is named after him, ask her about it."

Vittadini, who Rose had just met on his only trip to Uganda in 1985, also became very attached to her. "Look, in Rose, I think, there is the spirit of our movement. She is the charism of Father Giussani incarnated in a person. Certain things that I see in her, I have seen only in Mother Teresa. I remember when Mother Teresa came to Milan, to San Siro stadium in 1977. They asked her who the poor were for her. And she said: 'The poor are Jesus.' Period. There was nothing left to add. And that's how Rose is. She speaks about Christ as if he were her friend, without any affectation."

So he became for her, little by little, with time. But in those two years she spent in Italy, after the encounter with Father Giussani, the seed had already been planted.

Rose returned to Uganda in October 1992. Her formation in the hospital was finished, and the time was ripe to open a Memores Domini house in Kampala. Luisa Cogo, an elementary school teacher who took a leave from her Italian school, another companion from Varese, went with her. "During the first years in the Kampala house there were many changes," explains Broggi. "There was still no stable work. Those who went down there went to teach: they took two years of leave without pay and afterward returned to their job in Italy." The first to establish herself there would be Clara Broggi herself, who would go to Uganda four years later to work for AVSI.

In the meantime, Rose's world had changed a lot.

5

AIDS

> The infection spreads itself without recognizing any geographic, political, social, economic, or religious boundaries. But does the fact that young, old, mothers, children come to me with the symptoms and then die in front of me leave me without hope? Families are destroyed; tribes and traditions are destroyed; desperation, great confusion, fear, and suspicion spread themselves between man and woman, boy and girl . . . because there is no cure for the disease and the person finds himself without defense and without power in front of the virus. . . . . It is amazing that the whole society and the whole world, in depth, and we ourselves cannot look reality in the face…If we are sincere, if we start from a human position, we have to ask ourselves: What is this all about? What is the meaning of life, of love, and of death? Without this awareness, we cannot help ourselves let alone others.

RE-READING THEM now, these seem like words written a few months ago in the midst of the Covid pandemic. Instead, Rose said them in 2001, in front of the crowd at the Rimini Meeting. She was speaking about the reality that she has faced now for some time. The situation is the same today: a virus that sows death and fear, everywhere. The effects as well, and they go beyond the victims: they change human relationships, turn our way of living upside down, open up enormous questions. What is different, though, is the cause. It was not the coronavirus, but AIDS.

The Acquired Immune Deficiency Syndrome explodes at the beginning of the 1980s. It is a disease caused by a virus, HIV, that threatens the immune system and destroys white blood cells. The body no longer has any defenses: it is exposed to infection, it gets sick from any little thing, loses strength, and dies. The passage from being HIV-positive to AIDS is not automatic: often it does not happen or develops years later. But the fact that HIV can be transmitted through sexual relations and exchange of bodily fluids (and from the blood from syringes used by drug addicts), as well as through childbirth and breastfeeding, multiplies the fears. And the lack of treatment, at least at the beginning, made that fear a nightmare: more than two million people a year in the world would come to die from AIDS.

The newspapers began calling it "the Plague of the year 2000": a global epidemic that for a good decade united rich and poor, stars like Rock Hudson and Freddie Mercury and millions of poor people, before the discovery of antiretroviral treatment and the disparity between those who could access them and those who could not.

Many of the victims were from the so-called Global South. A lot of them in Africa where AIDS, according to the UN, became "a catastrophe." And while many of the sub-Saharan African countries tried in every way to hide the disease, trim the data and deny the evidence, Uganda did not. "Here, when the epidemic arrived, they talked about it publicly," recalls Rose. "In other places, where they were trying to protect tourism, they did not speak about it. But we did not have much to defend." The government moved quickly, she says. "They explained openly that AIDS existed and that it was transmitted in a certain way. They did an information campaign. The president accepted aid for research, for our doctors. He made it easy for those who wanted to come to give us a hand from outside." The result was that, in the 1990s, "the knowledge of the virus reached ninety percent even in the most faraway places. In other countries, there are still people that do not know that there is a treatment." The other side of the coin is that, along the way, the drama emerged in all its force.

The numbers are brutal. According to UNAIDS, the United Nations program addressing the epidemic, in 1990 (the first year that statistics were available), Uganda had an infection rate of 10.1% of the population between fifteen and forty-nine years old: 440,000 women and 93,000 children. There were at least 50,000 deaths, of which 19,000 were under fourteen years old. By the time Rose began her work, the true emergency was no longer war, but AIDS.

This emergency didn't just flood the hospital wards. In a talk a few years ago at the International Eucharistic Congress in Dublin, Rose described the situation like this: "In our country, you see on the street dozens of people that walk around aimlessly, others that are looking for something to eat. Many of the sick die after a long period of sickness in absolute poverty, without any help. So many children remain alone and without hope: after having seen their parents die like this, they end up on the street, looking for something to help them survive. Many of the victims, in the end, die of hunger."

The fallout from the disease was devastating. Rose had run across it in Italy while she was doing her training in Varese. The encounters with sick people are a constant part of her stories from these years: every time she speaks in public, she remembers facts, faces, words that have struck her. In her first talk at the August gathering of the 1991 Meeting, she got on the stage with Father Tiboni and Filippo Ciantia, a doctor from Varese and a missionary to Uganda from 1980 to 2009 and again in 2016. The theme of the discussion was the tenth anniversary of the presence of CL in Uganda. And Rose, asked to give witness to her experience, spoke about the first patients with AIDS that she met.

"Someone was brought to me that didn't even have a house and was forced to sleep under bridges," she recalled.

> He was thirty-six years old but looked like he was 100. For twenty years he had taken terrible drugs; in the winter he had to try to take shelter, but he didn't have anything with which to cover himself. Because of this he got sick with tuberculosis and the doctors had abandoned any hope. He was dirty and he smelled. I myself was terrified when I saw him. But I suddenly remembered that this man, dirty and sick as he was, was the presence, the sign of something greater. Destiny does not change. This person was not different just because he smelled and was sick with AIDS.

She spoke about the nurses who crept away, scared. About how she found herself alone with the patient: "and in looking at him I remembered the experience of Mary and John at the foot of the Cross." About how she struggled to carry that man to the bathroom, with the help of another sick person. "I started to wash him. I tried to put his feet in water, to cut his nails, his hair, his beard. I put new clothes on him that had been offered to me by a friend. Then I put him in a bed and gave him something to eat. While he ate, he asked me, 'Are you a sister?' I answered him, 'No, why?' 'Because you are not normal. You are doing things that the others do not do. Now I feel at peace, like I am at home again.' I answered him: 'Now, yes, you are truly at home and no longer alone. God has brought you to us. Now you belong to us.

You are a huge gift to me.'" That sick man died three days later. "But he died in peace, and I was sure that I had not wasted my time."

Another story, another encounter. "Giuseppe, a patient I met in Varese. When he arrived, he had been fighting with his parents; he didn't want to speak. And the doctors didn't know what to do. He had wounds all over. They had brought him into a room, and he did not speak; every doctor came, stopped and said: 'He is in a coma.' One day I went there. They had left an ointment on the nightstand; I took it and started to put it on his wounds. After two days, when I went to wash him again, he asked me: 'Who are you?' And I responded: 'So you do speak!' And he: 'Yes, I speak. For the doctors my case is a special case, they are all curious about my sickness, and I feel like a bunch of problems. But who am I? It is like I don't exist.'" A few days later, Rose was making her round of visits. "I was behind the other doctors, so much littler than they were. I made a sign and said: 'Ciao, Giuseppe!' And he: 'Ah! Ciao, Rose!' The doctors were amazed: 'Then you do speak!' And he: 'But she is my friend.'"

This is the gaze that Rose brought with her when she returned to Kampala and began to collaborate with AVSI, which was already present in Uganda. "In the main cities of the country there were Meeting Points built on the experience of people in CL: in Kitgum, in Hoima," recalls Ciantia. "The movement educates us to reckon with reality. There the reality was the AIDS epidemic, and so many of us set out to face it."

She set out to provide assistance to the poor and the sick. "But basically, I didn't know them," recalls Rose. "When I arrived from Italy, they said to me: 'Now you can begin working with the AIDS patients.' But there was nothing structured. I had to begin by myself. I thought to myself: 'What do I do: do I go knock on doors and ask if there are sick people?' It was something strange. But then I began to do something. I returned to the hospital in Nsambya, where I had studied. I worked there for free, because AVSI was giving me a salary. And then I went to the homes of the sick I had met in the hospital."

One day there was a patient who was particularly bad. "I accompanied him home. He continued to say, 'it's over there, over there,' but he was not telling me where. And at a certain point, I found myself in Kireka. When I arrived there, I received a shock. It was a very ugly place. There were just drunks, people fighting. And people died from their illness, in the street. So many of them had never even gone into the city. That was their world."

AIDS

Rose began to go to the slums often. Nagura, just past Kireka. "I went there to bring medicine to those who didn't have any. I asked for help from the hospital, and they gave me drugs and vaccines for the children." A little bit at a time, word of mouth spread. "At the hospital, I did counseling for those who had the HIV test; I helped those who received the results and stayed with the terminal patients. This was how I met people. And out of this came the first Meeting Point," which worked in collaboration with those in other cities.

It was an intense period, a time when the first house of the Memores in Uganda was also started. "They had a small apartment, close to AVSI," recalls Clara Broggi. "Later there were four women, and they rented another house, a little bit bigger, on the same street." The presence of the movement took shape; the NGO grew. And Rose's experience deepened.

She recounted her story as it happened because they were always asking her to write or to speak on some occasion. In *Traces*, in April 1994, an article of hers came out that is worth sharing again almost whole, because it says much about her and about her world. The title: "The Encounters of Rose."

> In the beginning, I was afraid of working at the Meeting Point. It was the fear of sacrifice. I knew that if I went to do the same work in the hospital, I would have found everything already in some way organized. There, instead, I had to be the one to invent the work, to wander around the city. Every morning, I prayed to be available to those whom the Lord put in front of me. In this way, Meeting Point assumed a much wider horizon: not only the care of those sick with AIDS, but the whole world, the desire to embrace the world as it is. Now I am happy, because this surrender to the Lord has made it possible for his design to reveal itself in the day and has allowed great, unimaginable things to happen. Like the conversion of Michele who, after having been with us a week, asked—he who was a Muslim—to be baptized because, "I desire to die embraced by your companionship."

There follows a roundup of small facts of extraordinary importance, even in their radical simplicity.

> A little while ago, during the Mass of the movement, three children received Baptism: Rose, the child of a woman I met while she was giving birth alone in the middle of the street. Ivan, a six-month-old orphan, who we found malnourished and covered with wounds. And Jacqueline, a ten-year-old child with a tumor that

> paralyzed her limbs. Another six people, adults and children, will be baptized soon. Among these there is the witch. Ancilla, this is her true name, was a true and proper witch. She did magic, worshipped sheep, and had a face that was so dark that at first I was afraid of her. I met her when I went to see her granddaughters, Harriet and Prisca, who were seriously sick. When Harriet died, I said that in that house God had to win and not the sheep. A few days later, the animals died, and the sister of the witch began to say that maybe, if they had died, they were not real gods, and my God was the true one. From that moment, I began to teach the catechism. Little by little, even Ancilla began to listen to me: and when she saw little Rose, at whose birth I had helped, she was moved and said: "For sure, your God is strange."

But it is what she writes a few lines later that shows how her horizons had already expanded past sickness.

> We were working with the crazy people who live on the street, the lepers, the handicapped, the children from the reformatory, the orphans to whom I taught Father Giussani's *The Religious Sense*. But all this happens because of the desire to communicate what we have met. When I began to go to the reformatory, where there are 270 young people, many were saying to me that it was impossible to change anything in that environment. They were wrong, because we do not want to change the situation, but to communicate what has happened. It is the change of people that characterizes the encounters that I have. This makes me discover my nothingness, because I know that I have not changed them. The only thing that I have to do is let myself be used by the Lord.

There is a lot there. A whole lot, if we think that she had basically just started. Above all, there is already this solid certainty: the individual is much more than "a sick person." A woman with HIV is not only her wounds, her swollen stomach, the weakness with which she falls to the ground while she drags water and is not even able to move herself from her straw mattress to give something to eat to the children who are looking at her. A gaze that stops there, at those wounds to be healed, is not sufficient.

"I am not that one particular aspect: I am not my sickness and that's it, AIDS and that's it," Rose explains. "In the hospitals, so many times, they treat sickness as a thing, as a table with a broken leg; you repair the leg and off they go. If someone has a bad eye, you heal only the eye: you see only the eye, not the *whole* man with his eyes. But man *is* a whole: he is a totality, with all his factors. If you are behind me and you touch my hair, I turn around, not only my hair turns around. It is the whole person that reacts. And the more serious the problem is, the more the totality is implied."

An approach that seeks only technical solutions to problems, even though this is indispensable, is not enough. "When AIDS appeared in Uganda, the minister of health put out publications that said: 'Make love, but be careful: be faithful, love only one person, and stay always with the same partner,' Rose remembered during her speech from 1991. These are reasonable precautions and even close to the position of the Church, compared to the campaigns of prevention based only on the diffusion of condoms. "But I realized that all this is useless, if one does not discover the reason for living. Life loses its value, its meaning. Families are divided. When a reason does not exist, life and work become a huge chaos. Everything appears as if it were hanging over a void."

And this void cannot be filled with "doing." Rose is very clear about this: "We who work in the medical field very often are tempted to consider health as the result of our personal efforts or of our science." She goes on: "The first day that I worked in the hospital, my desire was to cure every patient. But I discovered soon that the point was not this, and that, first of all, it was impossible. Men and women come to me constantly with their questions. And the true answer was that what we were doing was not due only to the medicines we could give them, but to the attention, to the love we also gave them. They came to us because they discovered something greater. It is beautiful to feel ourselves loved: it makes the sick people feel at home. The more they are happy, the more I myself feel happy, because they help me to encounter Christ. I am the one in need of the others; I am the one in search of him."

It is a maturity in her vocation that is first lived out in the house of the Memores. But there are other important relationships: the Italians of the Fraternity in Uganda and the Ugandan friends who share her work. One, Betty Birabwa, is still with her thirty years later, working at Meeting Point. "One of my acquaintances worked with the Comboni sisters: she introduced me to Father Tiboni and through him I met Rose. Since then, we have been good friends; we share the same challenges."

The other strong bond, obviously, was Tiboni himself, who became a great support in Rose's work as well. "He was a splendid person," remembers Betty.

He encouraged us, guided us in life. But above all, he taught us to value ourselves in order to be able to help others. He told us to ask ourselves always, in front of the sick: "And if it were me?" This helped me so much. Once we were at Seguku [a neighborhood southwest of Kampala] to meet a patient. There was this woman who was dying: she was very weak, she had diarrhea. There were two children with her, and one was just born. It was terrible situation, and I wanted to run away. That time it seemed like there was nothing to do. But then the words that "Tibo" had said to me came into my mind: "And if it were me?" We managed to do what we could to help her. Tiboni taught us to identify ourselves with the sick person, always. Otherwise, you cannot help.

This way of doing things expands to another work. Some members of the CL community began to go to the Reformation House, the house where there were dozens of orphans and kids from the street found by the police—in conditions that are hard to imagine. They do it as a charitable work, one of the cardinal points of Father Giussani's teaching: to dedicate time in a stable way to a gesture of charity. It is not only about doing good, but about learning an attitude, a way of treating others and reality. "Charity is the law of existence" is one of the phrases of Giussani that still marks generations of adults and young people educated in this gesture. In the context of Kampala—and in the life of Rose—it is so intertwined with her work that it is difficult to distinguish.

In *Traces* for November 1994, there appeared "a conversation of Father Giussani with some adults in CL." The title was, "A home in the World." Father Gerolamo Castiglioni, one of the leaders of the movement, recounts:

> Seven days ago, a letter arrived for Father Giussani from our friend Gloria, who is on mission in Kampala. In the *Memores Domini* house with Rose and a few others, she is dedicated to the care of those sick with AIDS: 'Dearest Father Giussani, the impact with Africa has been very dramatic because of the poverty and misery in which the common people live. Nothing comes easily to me, and in certain moments I have felt the impossibility of staying in front of these people who are sick, dirty, without the least hygienic conditions. One morning, when I said hello to Rose, she said to me: "Pray to Our Lady so that today you will not be afraid to see how Christ will present himself to you." With these words in my heart, I went with Claudia to the youth prison. Everything disgusted me: from the smell, to the dirtiness, to the scabies, to the lice. And at that moment, thinking again about Rose's words, I understood

that the question coincided with the position of my person, with my gesture. To be there, in front of them, sharing what little we could, coincided with my begging for Christ; between the begging and the gesture there is nothing in between. This is the climate of the house.

Father Giussani himself, a little further on, comments: "The letter of our dear friend Gloria helps us again to pass through the whole development of our spiritual, intellectual, and affective efforts, which represent our common life and thus, before all else, our personal life. . . . She tells us that the only question is to love, to want the good. How could we start out wanting the good without admitting and recognizing that the good is at the bottom of every being, is present in every moment, and more still, became the subject of an event in which He died for us? How can we desire the good without admitting that at the origin of everything, moment by moment, there is the Father, who sustains everything?"

It is from this way of acting that the Meeting Point spread out, attracting people and attention. The sick people that Rose and those who helped her to care for them were always increasing. People sought Rose out. AVSI provided support, and the word spread among the hospitals. Medicine arrived. Distance adoptions from Italy began. And aid to the families, to the children of those women who are sent to school, to the husbands who need to find work, multiplied. In the middle of the 1990s, the Meeting Point of Kampala was much more than a success story.

In the April 1996 issue of *Traces*, there is a report from Uganda by Renato Farina.[13] He writes: "Comparable to the air that is breathed where Rose Busingye and her companions are, there is only, in my opinion, the experience of Mother Teresa of Calcutta. Whoever meets the young women of the Memores Domini house in Kampala notices that it has to be God himself who is incarnate in this place. And whatever you've done before, whatever religion you've embraced: here is a place for you."

He describes the house of the women: "minuscule, in the midst of streets that smell of excrement and petroleum, where there is no security for anyone. And yet they are secure, in peace." And he reports a series of impressive facts. The story of Kintu, twelve years old, who was found in the reformatory "absolutely mute, not even a sound came out of his mouth" after he saw his mother and father killed by soldiers when he was four years old. "I brought him out and put him in our house for orphans. Now he goes to school. He was without hope of recovering his voice," recalls Rose. One night, all of a sudden, he started speaking again. After years. And after the prayer to Saint Riccardo Pampuri which she and her friends had begun to say for him.

Farina defines it as a miracle: maybe technically it is not, but it leaves one speechless. Like the story of Phillies "who spoke only the Alur language. She was surrounded by six beautiful children, but her cheeks were marred by shingles." They go to visit her—her sister is there at home with her, also named Rose: "She has babies on her knees and an English text of Father Giussani to be translated into Alur. What moments! Rose Busingye touches her gently. And Phillies has the other Rose translate: 'What I have understood is that man, woman, my children, you who listen will be called "I am not alone." Everything is entrusted to the Lord. Everything in him is companionship and joy. To my children I say: "I am going to another place. But I leave you God."' And she points to her Christian friends."

These are things from another world. And yet, during those same weeks, there was something revealing itself under the surface. Certain relationships had begun to wear thin, even with people from the movement: Ugandans and Italians. Rose doesn't stop to talk about this, because "it is not worth it: it weighed on me, it made me suffer.... But that was not the real problem."

The point was something else.

> I recognized more and more that what I thought was enough was not enough. We brought medication to the sick; we set up their therapies. We made charts for them, and they filled them out. But the day after you returned, the medicine had been thrown in the trash. And yet they knew what those medicines were for. Or, the money that you had given to someone so that he could eat got used to get drunk on *waragi*. The poor that we helped were complaining all the same. We found the children we had sent to school in the trash heap again; they preferred to stay there or to go around stealing. I thought: "How is this possible? You are sick, you are dying, I bring you medicine that will save your life, and you throw it away?"

Little by little, Rose entered a deep, difficult crisis. "Every day, I saw people dying or people who were lying to me. Even among my friends. But what I studied, what I had planned, was not like this. I arrived at the point where I wanted to escape. Truly: I wanted to leave, to go to a desert island where there was nobody. Only the insects." And it was in a moment like this that one evening, in the Memores house, the phone rang.

6

The Crisis

IT WAS FATHER Giussani calling the house in Kampala. He knew of Rose's difficulties. She spoke to him about her efforts, which she describes today like this: "You know when you realize that you are running after a thing, but you never manage to lay hold of it? This is how it was. At the end of the day, all that was left was tiredness. Even Jesus made me tired: it seemed like his legs were too long for me to keep up. I asked myself: then who is this people for me? And what am I truly? To whom do I belong? To the Africans, to the Italians, to the Memores?" These are not the exact words she used in that conversation with Giussani, but what really surprised her were the words that she heard in response. Father Giussani did not give her directives or spiritual advice; he just asked her to do one thing: "Stop everything and come to Italy. And buy a one-way ticket. I will send Pier Alberto to pick you up."

Pier Alberto Bertazzi was one of the leaders of the movement (to him and to other university students we owe the title of the 1969 flyer that named Communion and Liberation) and of Memores Domini. A doctor with a sharp mind and great discretion, he died just a few years ago, in September 2021. Giorgio Vittadini maintains that he was one of the most important figures for Rose, "because of how he accompanied her: he served her with absolute humility, in the name of Giussani first and then in the name of Julián Carrón, his successor," and she confirms this.

But to that amazing request of Giussani, she gave a surprising answer: a decisive "no." "I thought he hadn't understood what I was doing," she explains. "'He didn't understand the children, he didn't understand the sick people, he didn't understand this, he didn't understand that.' And in that moment, I told him no, that I couldn't go: to close the Meeting Point did not seem right."

Bertazzi arrived in Kampala a few days later, but to no effect. Rose was not convinced. She spoke to him about her problems, her struggles. She told him about certain relationships that were showing some cracks. But she did not budge. The Italian doctor would leave a few days later, alone. She stayed there, with her anxiety. "I said to myself: 'Why Italy? Why should I close down? It is not right. I am correct not to go.' But there was something that didn't feel right."

That "something" exploded suddenly one night. Rose recalls it: "I couldn't sleep. I turned here and there; I was full of thoughts and couldn't fall asleep. I thought, I thought. . . . At a certain point—it was more or less four in the morning—I remember that this thought came all of a sudden into my mind: 'Are you there, Jesus? If you are here, let's go!' I got up, went to the phone, and called Father Gius: 'I am coming.'"

Rose smiles while she tells this story. She says that the trip to Milan, at the beginning of July 1996, was full of apprehension, like when you go to an exam knowing that you are not prepared, and you look for plausible excuses, first of all for yourself. "I prepared speeches for Giussani. I was expecting him to ask me: 'Why did you not come right away?' and I wanted to have my justifications ready. 'They told me this. . . . They did this. . . .' An eighteen-hour trip like this."

Those fears were deflated as soon as she arrived at Linate Airport. Father Giussani was there waiting for her. He hugged her. He didn't ask her anything, only "How are you?" And then: "Let's go to lunch!"

It is not far from Linate airport to Sacro Cuore, a school near the Lambrate neighborhood on the periphery of Milan: a very large institution, with different locations. It is the only school run directly by CL because Giussani himself wanted it as a place that would exemplify his educational method. There is a residential wing in the building with apartments. There for a good six months, Father Giussani—among the thousand commitments and problems that came from his guidance of a movement that was present in many countries—went, as often as he could, to meet Rose to do the simplest thing in the world: to spend a few hours with her. A walk, lunch, a talk.

"The day after I arrived, he came to meet me, and we were there in the garden," Rose remembers. "I was still waiting for him to scold me: 'Why didn't you come?' And instead, no: he told me about his life, talked about himself, about the movement. We talked. This was all he did, for six months."

He spoke above all about himself. Rather, about his experience, about what he had learned—what he was learning—little by little from reality. Learning from reality is one of the cornerstones of the founder of CL's charism. "One day he said to me: 'You know, Rose, soon after the movement began, everyone left. I was alone in the dark, in a tunnel. But at a certain point something happened: I began to say "I." And it was as if a small light began to come on. I went out of the tunnel, and in the end, I found three other friends. With those three, the movement began again.' And while he spoke about the darkness, it was like a replay of my life, of that night when I had said: 'Jesus, are you there?'"

Those were crucial months. Every time she talks about herself, Rose mentions that time, returns there. It was not only hearing the words of Giussani: it was his presence, his way of seeing, of doing, of living. "Christianity, in the end, is a man who is full of joy, who pulls you along, and you desire to be happy like him," says Rose. "Moreover, it is not even like you want to: you enter into that wave of joy. Like a wind that carries you along, and you are there inside it. You could see how he enjoyed wine. It is not that you set out thinking: 'I will drink too, but maybe it will be bad for me? And who knows how it will taste.' No, seeing the way he held the glass, you held it that way. And you found that you had already drunk and had made a new discovery. Like a beautiful wind. A whisper that carries you. But it corresponds to what you are. And it makes you discover who you are."

As Nacho Carbajosa says, "That point for her was fundamental. The brilliant pedagogy of Giussani—this 'don't talk over,' but 'be together'; don't attack the problem directly, but help someone simply follow the fascination of what you have found, and then face everything, even the problems—is also decisive for understanding what happened later, when Rose returned to Uganda."

But another factor, more subtle but equally important, helps us understand the whole dynamic that developed from then on, especially with the women: it is the concept of *belonging*. It is not simply being connected to a reality—to the Church, to the movement, to a friendship—but precisely the discovery, thanks to that reality and to a definite relationship, of belonging *structurally* to someone, of belonging to God. "I looked at Father Gius and thought to myself: if a man looks at me like this, with this capacity to love, what about God?" It was in this sense that the bond with Giussani opened up an even more radical discovery for her: "It was as if, through him, God was saying to me: you are mine, you belong to me."

It is rare to listen to Rose speak, privately or publicly, without hearing the word "belonging," without returning to that discovery: I know *who I am* when I discover *whose I am*. "A man becomes a protagonist in reality, and reality becomes his, when he discovers whose he is, not only who he is," she will say, for example, in one of her most beautiful talks at the Rimini Meeting in 2007. "My experience was like this: when I had someone who told me 'You are mine,' I began to live, I began to glimpse a meaning. It was as if a light had illuminated everything; I began to discover the truth about my life."

And the next year, again on the stage in Rimini:

> You become lord of reality not because you possess it, but because you discover that it is made by Another, because it depends on a design that is not yours. For us, it is this discovery of a paternity in action, within the events of our day, of our existence, that makes life a dance, such that one can fly even in spite of sickness and death. Our little I is just like a breath: it can never be a protagonist unless there is this belonging; without belonging you grab here and there at what happens and at what you are able to take; you remain unstable and uncertain. When you lose the value of belonging, you also lose the value of yourself; and you lose the meaning and the value of everything else, your I and your personality are in crisis. Instead, belonging to Christ, to the Church, for us, became the experience of a bond that redefines us forever and that manifests itself in everything we are and do.

Another important moment was the testimony that Rose gave at the Macerata-Loreto pilgrimage which CL from the Marche region organizes yearly as a gesture of (at the last pre-Covid pilgrimage, more than 90,000 people walked twenty-seven kilometers through the night to the Marian shrine). Rose participated in it in 2010 and was invited to speak before the departure from Macerata. She spoke of what happened to her when she was with Father Giussani:

> I began to live and to work when I knew concretely how to respond to the question "Whose am I?" When this question ("Whose am I?") had precise faces, with first names and last names, I became free. Paradoxically, I became free by belonging, that is, by having a bond. When you are free, you can finally be in front of all reality without fear. I became free because someone revealed to me who I am. It was evident that I was nothing, and yet I felt that I was

embraced and desired. It was as if Giussani's gaze said to me: "You have an infinite value." From that gaze, everything was born. In that gaze, in fact, I discovered that I am not defined by my limits, but that the personal relationship with which God makes me exist constitutes me as an infinite desire for him. That gaze of belonging to Christ and to the Church . . . was the content and method of my work: to communicate the love for the unbounded greatness of existence of each person and to offer to that person the same companionship toward destiny that embraces my life."[14]

When she speaks about it again today, Rose synthesizes everything in two sentences. "Father Giussani made me discover my value. From there, it was like an airplane taking off." And she makes a hand gesture that rises up and takes flight.

She had arrived in Milan in July 1996. She left for Uganda at the end of November of that same year. There she met Clara Broggi, who had moved to Kampala just before Rose left. "We had seen each other for just a day. I was arriving in Uganda, and she was leaving for Italy. I spent my first six months there, until just before Christmas, without Rose. But when she arrived, she was a completely different person. Much more sure of herself." In what sense? "If before, for example, Tiboni said something, she was all in; if someone else said something different, she let herself get confused and didn't understand anymore which way to go. Now, instead, she was certain; she knew what her path was. And no one could have stopped her. Even with Tiboni, for example. She always treated him like a father, but at the same time she began to make certain observations, to tell him more of her own thoughts: 'This doesn't seem right to me. . . .' Before she would never have done that. And this change was very recognizable. She told Tiboni: 'Now I know who I am.'"

It was a new awareness of herself, which also informed her way of working, of approaching the sick. The people were the same, even the problems: sickness, misery, children. "But I had discovered my worth; I was certain of that. I don't know how to say it, but when I said to others, 'Look, you have an infinite value,' it was an experience that I was having for myself. The words weren't different, but the experience was." And the people, in some way, understood it. They saw this experience in flesh and bone—and then as something concrete, something possible for them to live as well. Even in front of AIDS, or death.

At the Rimini Meeting in 2003, Rose would share an example that was significant. She was speaking about Fiona, ten years old, HIV-positive and sick with AIDS.

> She was dying of meningitis and was the only child left in her family; everyone had died of AIDS; the family was over. There was only this little child left. Once, when I came to her in bed, she said to me: "I don't want to die like my mom, I want to live. Help me live for two months, help me live for a year; I want to go to school and play with my friends." When she spoke to me like this, I couldn't sleep, I wasn't able . . . I had only a little money for treatment. I told this to a doctor and to those in my house, and so we decided to do an antiviral treatment. But we didn't have much money, and the other doctors laughed, because you have to start when you have all the medicines for your whole life. But I thought: what does it matter, if only I can give a month to this child, if I can give her two months or a year to live, so she can find an answer to her desire. But for me the first desire was that this child could discover that she was something great, that her life was important. We began the treatment. After two weeks, the girl began to get out of bed, and after another two weeks they discharged her.

Fiona then returned to school. Rose explained, "I thought that when one begins to say 'I,' she sees things in a different way, begins to glimpse the meaning of life; when you know whose you are, greatness can happen anywhere. It can happen and *happens* anywhere. It can happen even when I am stuck in the mud, as always happens, or when I am under the sun that burns my head, or when I am in front of my car with a flat tire that has to be changed. Greatness can happen as well in front of a child like William, who was afraid of dying and said to me: 'Look, all I ask is this: hold my hand when I have to die, hold my hand firmly, so that I am not afraid of dying.' In fact, when he died, he died in my arms."

7

The Women

"LOOK, THAT IS the cauldron." Ketty's home is at the end of a narrow alley in Kireka, three minutes from Meeting Point. You turn the corner, walking by a short wall, and see a mother and two children on the other side of the gutter, hanging clothes and looking curiously. We arrive in front of a brick cube that is not very big, with a door that has an iron lock. Ketty gives a couple turns of the key, says "enter" with a smile, and opens her world to you. Everything is all enclosed in one room, four meters long and three meters deep, and in the back, a curtain separates one room from another area that you don't see, but that you can't imagine is much bigger. A dresser, a small TV, a few furnishings. A tiny window. A frying pan. And placed on the rough cement pavement, to the right of the entrance, there is a large pot, supported by another kind of pot for boiling spaghetti, but full of white ashes. "What they had me use in the bush was like this: I walked around with two sacks on my back, and I carried on my head a big pot with the stuff I would cook." She makes gestures, miming. But it is difficult to imagine what it was really like. She touches her hair. "I had a spot up on top where there wasn't any more hair. All burned." Ketty looks you in the eyes while she speaks, but it is as if her gaze occasionally passes beyond, through you, to see the ghosts of her past.

She was one of the women who appeared in the exhibit for the Meeting of Rimini in 2021. In the first room of the exhibit, there was a video: "Chapter 1: Darkness." The clip showed her in the foreground, alternating with a few full-length cuts while she was sitting, and the story flowed out, in front of dozens of faces that became more and more moved. She also spoke about the cauldron; but you can't really imagine it, until you see it there. And until she made those motions, as if she had to put it on her head again.

That video—by Emmanuel Exitu, the director of *Greater*—is entitled *The Queens of Kampala*. And it is true: Ketty and the others, Rose's women, are truly queens, in this strange kingdom made of nothing, but where the person is everything. When a guest arrives at Meeting Point, like me, they welcome him with forty-five minutes of songs and dances. These women have a magnificent power, a will to live that comes out while the music and drums keep the tempo. There are at least forty of them in the courtyard under the canopy. Rose is seated on the steps in front of them, with her usual baseball cap and a light scarf around her neck. Next to her, other women watch, laugh among themselves, keep track of the little children that slip away onto the pavement on all fours and every so often get dangerously close to the dances. On the side, there are some faces looking over the fence. It seems like a party. It is a party.

There is a song that the women often perform. It is called "When I Met Rose," and the women wrote it, adding verses little by little. It is the story of their life. The group of women is in the background, singing in choir. Two or three of them, in turn, come forward, and sing out the words of the verse: "When I was a widow. . . . When I was a street kid. . . . When I was a crazy woman. . . ." And they mime a widow, a homeless person, a crazy woman. "Since I met Rose, she gave me back my heart and saved me. Rose set me free." And then in choir: "Free, now I'm free. Rose set me free." I am free now. Rose has given me back my heart and saved me. And they laugh and dance while the song goes on ten, fifteen, twenty minutes, and it seems like it will never stop, with those verses that are added on little by little, as other stories and other lives are added by the women of Kireka.

You get goosebumps hearing "When I was in the bush," when I was in the forest, taken by the rebels. Coming forward out of the group is Ketty, together with Agnes—she was also in Exitu's video. One plays the tormentor, the other the victim: bound, threatened with a knife, dragged like an animal. Until the cord is cut and Ketty suddenly gets up, with an unexpected agility, singing together with the choir: "I am free, Rose set me free." These two women really lived what they are now acting out. Knives, cords, blood. Death. All real, in their skin and then in their hearts, for years. What has made them so free that they can now relive the horror, and exorcise it, every time they perform that song?

When the dance finishes, they begin to introduce themselves. One by one. It has a different rhythm, this story. Slower than the way we introduce ourselves, less worried about getting through it quickly and passing on to the next person. Nothing is left implicit. An episode takes the time it needs, if it is important: it is explained in all its passages, even those that we would take for granted. And they repeat a dialogue to you without any rush, phrase by phrase, almost word for word: "And then she said to me. . . ." "And I answered her. . . ." It comes from inside. It takes a bit of getting used to. But then you find yourself immersed a bit at a time, without realizing it. And you recognize that in this slow flow, with the English that follows the sing-song tone used in these parts, each word has its place and its weight, even those that might seem superfluous to you. They are precious for them; they have been cut into their flesh, like scars. It is a gift they are giving you.

Ketty's last name is Akola Dong. She is from the North. She was a little over twenty years old and already a mother when she was kidnapped by rebels in 2001. She and twenty other people from her village. "One of us was pregnant, but she did not tell anyone because she was scared." Then began the march in the forest, where the guerillas would go continuously to avoid the army. And then the hell began.

> "When the rebels found out that that woman was pregnant and had trouble walking, they called another kid from the village and told him: 'Kill her.' He didn't want to, but they told him: 'Kill her, or we will kill you.' That boy took a machete and killed her. They forced him to cut her into pieces. Then they took those pieces and put them in a pot. And they forced us to eat, because we had to become strong."

She remained in the bush for a year and a half. They raped her. She contracted HIV. She became pregnant and then lost the baby. She suffered continual beatings, and a blade cut her on the back of a leg: the scar is there, along the tibia. They made her walk for hours, with that boiling pot balanced on her head. And given that she was strong, and knew the area, at a certain point they put her at the head of one of the gangs. "They gave me orders, and I had to execute them." That meant entering into a village, looting, killing. And doing it in her homeland, among her people. "Once they made me close the mouth of a woman with a padlock. They pierced her lips with a spike, and I put in the lock and closed it. But I was able to hide a copy of the key," and she brings her hand to her breast, miming the gesture. "Before we left, I gave it to her when they couldn't see me."

She started to feel the HIV little by little. "I continued to get weaker. I had trouble walking. They gave me drugs to keep me on my feet, but it got worse and worse." Then they left her behind, telling her, "We will return later to take you." It was her salvation. She stayed there, hidden. She found a man who knew her and brought her to her home. "Four days' journey, and I was afraid that he would kill me on the road. By then I no longer trusted anyone."

When she arrived at the village, she saw her mother and began to cry, "because she had thought I was dead." Her children did not recognize her: "I had no hair and looked old." But the rebels were still in that area. Ketty had to hide herself, and then decided to leave her children with her mother and flee to Kampala, where her sister lived.

She arrived on a truck, distraught. "I was too weak to walk. They brought me to the departure point in a wheelbarrow. I stank; I was covered in wounds; I didn't have any money. At the end of the trip, the driver was infuriated when I told him I couldn't pay him."

But someone had pity on her and brought her to the slum. Her sister and brother-in-law helped her as they could, then they kept her isolated, out of fear. "I had my cup, my little pot. In the evening, they brought me something. But I was getting worse and worse."

At that point, she learned about Meeting Point. And she began that road to rebirth that brings her to tell her story here today, overflowing with life, while she dances with an unexpected agility for a body that weighs eighty kilos, or speaks with her round, full face and a smile that only now and then shows a shadow of other things.

The story of Agnes Achan Aida comes later, at one of the tables of Meeting Point. She speaks in a very low voice, an effect of her sickness. She too has a gaze that is deep and full of life, with a veil of melancholy that comes often, while she recalls her story. It is very similar to Ketty's. She was kidnapped by rebels in 1997, "from a village on the border with South Sudan." Violence, infection. She remained in the forest for almost three years before she was able to return to a house which was no longer her home. Put simply, they no longer wanted her. "They told me all kinds of things: 'Look, here's the one who returned from the bush. She kidnapped our children, she is a killer, she cannot be with us.' Even my husband told me the same thing: 'You cannot stay here, go back to your family's house.'"

Agnes took the path of many who were uprooted by the violence of those years and went to Kampala. "I had an aunt, my father's sister, who lived in Naguru. I thought that maybe she could help me. But it is when you are with a person that you see how they really are. I stayed there for four months, but I was very sick. I didn't have any money, and I couldn't ask anything from them, not even medicine; and you know our hospitals, you know that if you go there without money no one will take care of you." She started to work in the market. "There was a woman from our village: I sold beans for her. But when I finished work, she did not pay me. The day after I went back, and she told me: 'Come back tomorrow.' I returned again: 'I don't feel good, you can see: I'm always sick, I need medicine.' And she told me simply: 'I will not pay you. And if you are going to kill me, like you did to those others in the bush, well, you can't do it here.' I was petrified. But it was not just because of the money and the medicine."

Even her aunt, a little later, distanced herself from Agnes. "She was afraid that I might infect her. She got another room for me in another house close by: they brought me food once a day. I could barely move to get to the door and take the food and water. Sometimes, I wasn't able to eat for three or four days, but they left me there. Until one day, I heard a knock, and it was the social worker. She came in and asked me how I was. I told her that I was sick and that I wasn't able to pay for medicine. She asked me if I had ever been in the hospital, and I told her that I didn't even know where the hospital was. She left, saying: 'I'll come back.' The next day she returned, and Rose was with her. It was the first time I saw her."

The story of this encounter is similar to so many others, and yet it is unique, like all the others.

> She came in and started speaking with me, as if she had always known me: you know when you talk with someone that you have never seen but she seems familiar? She just said to me: "Can I bring you to the hospital?" But inside I was saying: "No, I can't go." I was very pessimistic. I wanted to die. I thought that wherever I would go, people would look at me badly and wouldn't welcome me. I told her no. But she insisted: "Do not worry about the rest; I only want you to agree to come to the hospital: that is all I am asking of you." Then I told her: "OK." At the hospital they had me do all the exams, and they found out that I had tuberculosis. They took care of me, but I was so weak that I couldn't even stand up."

And Rose?

She was always with me: she came in the evening, she was there, she made sure that I ate, that I took my medicine. . . . Everything. Since I had returned from the forest, it was the first time that I had someone next to me who loved me. She didn't keep her distance. She came close, instead of distancing herself. I began to ask myself: "Who is this person?"

When they discharged her, Rose found her a place to stay.

She brought me to a house where there was a room all to myself. There was also a mattress: I didn't sleep on a mattress, I slept on the floor. "I want to be here." I began to think: "God, maybe You sent this person to protect me." But it was not enough for me; my head was still thinking about the past. Even though I had seen so many new things: there were the women from Meeting Point who came to cook and to clean my house. But I said to myself: "Maybe these people are looking for something from me. It is like the other organizations; at a certain point they will ask you for something." I still wasn't well.

One day, she recounts,

I took courage. I went to Rose and asked her: "Can you give me 20,000 shekels?" And she: "What do you need it for?" "I want to return home, to my village." She listened to me. She did not respond. She looked at me in silence, for many minutes. She had brimming eyes. And then she said: "Agnes, you have a value. You have an infinite value." I did not understand what she meant: when people spoke about value, I always thought that they meant important people, like a president, or someone who works for a big company. I didn't understand. But she told me: "I will not give you that money. Stay here. We prepared a place for you, and we will help you. If you have any problems, you can share them with me." And then she continued to repeat this thing about value to me.

Agnes did not leave.

I remained there, and she continued to come every day, to see how I was. But in my head, this "value" thing was still going around. I am not someone important, so I wasn't able to understand. These women came to help me, but they did not know who I was. And I continued to think that sooner or later they would ask me for something in exchange. Until one day, Rose came and told me: "Let's go, come meet these other women." "Where?" At that time, Meeting Point had already started up in Naguru. It was from there that these women were coming. I went there, but it seemed like it wasn't the right place for me. I remained sitting there in silence, thinking: "Why did they ask me to come here? These women don't have any problems, what does this have to do with me?" They sang, they danced, they spoke to each other. I thought that I was the only one there who had problems. Then I stopped going there. Rose came to ask me: "Why didn't you come to the meeting?" And I: "Those women don't have any problems." Because I saw how they laughed, how they were happy, while I wasn't happy at all. She only told me: "No, go." She didn't tell me anything about them.

Agnes was convinced. She returned. And that week, at Meeting Point, there was a guest. "The women danced and sang, to welcome him. They told me: 'You sing too, dance with us.' I was sitting there looking at them. Then they began to talk about their experiences. These women, who were dancing and singing and were happy, they had problems too. Big problems: AIDS, some were abandoned by their husbands, some didn't know how they were going to eat." In that moment, says Agnes, "something happened: I realized that maybe that was a place where even people who had very serious problems were able to be happy."

That evening, when she returned home, Rose came by: "How are you?" "Good." "Are you happy?" "And there I answered her: 'Yes, I am happy.' 'Now you are home,' she told me, 'The Meeting Point is your new home; you have a family that will take care of you.'"

Everything began very slowly, Agnes says: "But it was in this way that I began to understand who I am: my journey started from there. When I went to the meetings, I didn't grasp everything, but I drew out one or two things that helped me. It educated me. And every time I understood my value more. I began little by little. The journey was slow, slow, slow. Sometimes I go back a step. But I am happy. To discover myself is not something that happens in a day: I am still discovering it, and the journey is not over yet. And I think that I will continue to learn even more things until the end of my life."

If you ask her who Rose is for her, she thinks about it for a second. And, from the first word, she chooses something unexpected: "She is an educator. A teacher. She accepts the way you are, and she makes you understand who you are. Being with her and these women I learned many more things about myself, about work, about education, about all that I have received. Now I am free. I am happy. And I discovered two treasures that I will never forget, for my whole life: love and care. From the first day I encountered Rose, she showed me only this: love and care."

Now Agnes is a social worker at the International Meeting Point. "How important is it to work here? Incredibly important. It is not a question of money: it is the people with whom I work who are important for me."

Teddy Bongomin also works with her. She is fifty-two years old, has a beautiful round face and a colored streak in her hair. She was one of the first women of Meeting Point: "I have been here from the beginning." When she speaks about Rose, she says: "I wish I had met her sooner. I lost my parents when I was still young. I left school and got married because I thought marriage would make me happy. And I wanted to help my relatives, given that I was the oldest in the family."

But the first marriage did not go as she had hoped. Life began to be "a hell on earth: it did not answer my desire. I was still looking for true happiness." Then "Aunt Rose" began to work in her neighborhood. "She came to accompany a patient. After there came another two, three. . . . There were so many people who were suffering there, but there was also the need for a new heart." And the difference is this: "In that place, government officials came by, people from all the organizations, but no one really took care of the people in the slum. I called them 'the people with suitcases.' When you are in Kireka, you leave it with dirty shoes and the tires of your car covered in feces. The people who came would never return. Rose stayed. From the first moment to today."

And she allowed Teddy to make what she calls "the path of discovering who I am. Each of us can find a certain amount of peace, but if the awareness of yourself is lacking, you will continue to complain: your heart will never be in peace. All of us have to ask this simple question: 'Who am I?' In front of everything we face, we have to stop and ask ourselves: 'Who am I? And what are all these things that are in front of me? All the beauty that I see—the sun, the beauty of the morning—it is all for me. But who am I?' It is thanks to this question that I could even pass through torture. When my husband died, I found myself alone with my children. Then I began to ask myself: why is this woman like this? What makes her like that? When I found myself face to face with her, all these things disappeared. I began to want it for myself." Teddy says that having discovered her dignity is "the only thing that makes me happy. A human being needs this: if you give him this, the day after he forgets all the reasons he had to complain." And this is what happened to her.

Among Teddy's colleagues at Meeting Point there is Hanifa Namwesezi. She is not a social worker; she does the cleaning here. She has large eyes and a very sweet smile. She communicates with those eyes and that smile when she comes across any new guest. Her English is still not great; she never studied it. She met Rose and her women almost six years ago. "When I came to them, I didn't have any hope," she said once when they asked her to talk about herself. "I hated myself and my children." It was because of her poverty even more than her sickness. "We had nothing to eat, and we didn't have money to send our children to school. I was at home, closed in on myself, and we didn't do anything; the children were there with me, and they just slept. And when they woke up, they were always faint. I spent the time expecting nothing and asking myself when I would die. I watched my children walk in front of me and looked at them as if they were not mine, because I had nothing to give them." One of her kids ended up cutting himself with a knife, out of desperation.

When they spoke to her about Meeting Point, there were people who tried to dissuade her. "They told me: 'You are Muslim, you will see how they welcome you.' Instead, I found people who encouraged me. My life changed. And not because of money or anything else, but because of what they showed me."

One of the things that struck her was that

> they welcomed me to their table; I didn't expect this. I thought that the rich would sit with the rich and the poor with the poor. Instead, I saw that I could sit down and eat with them. But what surprised me even more was that they came to my house. I live in a small alleyway, in a poor house that has trash all around it. But they sat down and ate with me. This amazed me and made me happy. It made me understand that these people didn't look at the wealth but at the value of the person. The rich are rich and things are things; at a certain point, things run out, and even wealth. But the value of a person never runs out.

She told Rose about her children and her sickness, "and she comforted me: she told me that to be sick does not mean one is going to die. A little at a time I began to recover hope. Now my life is in order. The sickness seems almost just a memory. I don't feel it because I am happy. And even my children are happy."

It is striking to see her, a Muslim, show up to Mass sometimes. "When I went into a church and saw people praying, and the silence, I felt that God was there among us." And if they ask her why she goes to the CL meetings, she responds in all simplicity: "I am not able to follow many things. But there I seek love. I don't know English, but everything that comes from there helps me to know myself and other people. Maybe I manage to understand one word, but I work on that one word: because the words that come from there are words that give me life again."

When offered a job at Meeting Point, she was uncertain. "In the beginning, I refused. I didn't believe in myself, and I didn't think I would be able to do it. But Rose told me not to worry. Alberto [Repossi] sometimes tells me things that I don't understand or asks me to do something and I do the opposite, but he continues to have patience with me. When I began to work here, my life changed. We have food; we have drink. And we are happy. To be happy, a person does not need money or a bunch of stuff: everything depends on knowing who you are. This is the greatest thing that I learn from Meeting Point International."

It seems impossible that all this could ultimately come from those six months of walks and talks in a garden on the outskirts of Milan. And yet it is true. That "plane that took off," set everything in motion, transforming something that was already enormous—with the facts as they have been recounted so far—into something else.

"I understood what was not right in the women, why they did not take their medication," says Rose. "Giussani always pointed me back to my value. He made me discover that. You don't have to wait for other people to figure it out: I am the one who has to discover it. I have to discover that Christ is the life of my life, in flesh, in bone. To discover Jesus within me." And that change permeates the relationship with the women. "The things that I say to them are not very different from the things that I said before. I also spoke about value before, about the importance of what they have inside them. I explained to them all the good reasons they had to take care of themselves. But they were explanations. Maybe they weren't really mine, deep down." Afterwards, they were.

In one of the public testimonies, a while ago, she put it like this: "In the relationship with Father Giussani, I found my greatness again: I discovered that the human being is a relationship, and this relationship makes her someone. My desire from that time was to make others understand, despite their weakness and their sickness and their sin, that they are great, to help them know that they are greater than their limits. My friend made me understand that humanity is small, is almost nothing in front of the cosmos, seems like a penny, like a breath: but the world has value because there is humanity. All the other values of the world have to be at the service of the individual person, little as she is."

These are the identical words she says now: "The unhappy person is the one who decides that it is impossible to be happy. I began to desire that all people would understand this: that they are greater than what we can imagine. Then my work became one of forming a relationship in which each person I encounter could discover that they are someone, that is, could discover his value and his dignity." Period. Nothing more.

One of the women about whom Rose often speaks is Lucy. Rose met her a little after her return to Uganda. The rebels had raped Lucy and stuck a padlock on her vagina, to stop anyone else from going out with her. Then they took out her teeth and cut off a piece of her nose. Before she arrived in Kampala, she had been in a refugee camp in the North. "At a certain point she told me: 'For others, I am just a load of problems; they come and ask me what the rebels did to me, where they cut me. But who am I? I am like a basket where you throw out the trash; but I, as Lucy, who am I?'" Rose says that she couldn't find any words. She embraced her. And then: "Yes, you are all this drama, this disfigured face. But you have a greater value. It seems like you only these problems, but for me you are worth infinitely more." Lucy began to attend the encounters at Meeting Point. "One day she told me: 'Rose, I want to live because you are here. You have given me a value.' And I answered her: 'No, Another has given you your value. Another wants you to exist.'"

Looking at Ketty, Agnes, Hanifa, and the others, in the end this is what you see. Nothing other than this discovery. "In the last years, when I have gone to Uganda, we have had an assembly with the women," says Father Nacho Carbajosa. "You ask questions, you speak about life. But it strikes me that in one way or another they always return to this: there is One who makes me exist now. Anyone who has read Father Giussani and *The Religious Sense* knows that for him this awareness is 'the keystone' of religiosity. But for them it is not a phrase from a book: it has entered into them."

The life of the two centers, Naguru and Kireka, is identical. Rose passes by each one twice a week. One morning she meets with the women. They talk about any problems or simply tell her about themselves, about the experiences they have had. Depending on the needs that come out, or on those who have just recently arrived, they organize small classes. Above all English, hygiene, and nutritional education. "We look together at how they cook or how they clean their house," says Rose. "It is not difficult to introduce new things: within the friendship, they trust, they understand quickly that these things are useful to them." From the sewing classes, ten years ago, there came one of the activities that helps them to live, together with the rocks: they sell homemade bags and shirts. The women also come in the afternoon for meetings with the social workers.

Two young men serve as night guardians. "One is Vincent. He goes to the university and lives here because his parents died and he had nowhere to go," says Rose. "The other is Kintu, who is famous because he was mute and then through prayers to Saint Riccardo Pampuri was able to speak." They also work out sometimes. They were playing a lot of soccer, before Covid stopped everything, but they will probably start again soon. There is a small nurse's station, a doctor who comes by at least every fifteen days, because more than half of the women and a good number of their children have HIV. Those little offices are the only thing that makes you think about sickness. Looking at the women, it would never come to mind. "One time, a few officials from the UN came and they did not believe us: 'It is not possible that these women are sick,'" Rose recalls.

Not always, but often, the gatherings close with a walk in the slum. It is not the only walk: before the pandemic every now and then the same column of women could be seen leaving for a ride in a broken bus to Lake Victoria or one of the green valleys that you find just outside the city. "We do it to discover beauty, because ugliness does not define us," explains Rose. "What defines us is Beauty with a capital 'B.'"

"There is a relationship among the women that goes beyond clan and family ties," observes Repossi. "And this generates, brings growth. But it happens because Rose lives this way with them. She continues to say, 'It doesn't matter what tribe you are from.' In fact many times they have to translate at their gatherings, because the ones who speak Acholi don't speak Luganda, etc. But there is a bond that goes beyond language and tribe." It affects the work groups and becomes a reciprocal support: to take care of the other's kids when one is at the quarry or in the hospital for treatment. Or to host someone who gets evicted. Even to take care of the orphans or a child found on the street.

This is not a rare case: Rose remembers a list of stories and names from way back. In Rimini in 2003, speaking about the daily life of the "new" Meeting Point International, she said: "My sick people adopted a kid last year who was sixteen years old; despite the limits of their sickness, of their poverty, they have a desire for happiness for themselves and want others to be happy as well. When this kid became an orphan, he was kicked out by the owner of the house they were renting. I was not there; and yet the women went out, one giving 100 shekels, another gave another 100. . . . And when I returned, they told me: 'You can relax. This kid is ours; we will take care of feeding him and paying the rent.' This doesn't happen even for one who earns thousands of shekels. Sometimes the sick contribute their money to bring other sick people to the hospital, to pay for their medicine—because here we have to pay for everything. You ask yourself: 'Why do they do it?' It is because they have discovered that, despite their limits, their poverty, their sickness, they have found happiness, and they want others to be happy too."

The bond touches even the way they treat money. One of the fruits of their financial education are savings groups and loans for microbusinesses. A share of the revenues is put in a common account, and those who are enrolled can ask for a small loan to buy something they need for their house or help to start a small business: the sale of mangos, potatoes, *chapati*, a kind of flatbread like a Mexican tortilla. The groups govern themselves: there is one who keeps the accounts, and the loans are repaid a little at a time. Self-managed microcredit, in short. In general, it works, sometimes it doesn't.

"Look, these women are not saints," says Repossi. "They still make mistakes. Every now and then someone plays tricks. Many have men in their lives and children from different fathers. Sometimes the husbands steal. They fight, they betray, they leave each other. But even the person who does this almost always returns. It is another thing Rose repeats: 'We have the idea that a Christian has to be better. In reality, the Christian remains the same: she makes mistakes, like everybody, because we are all sinners. And yet she knows at some level that she can always return.'"

Three or four years ago, Repossi recalls, one of the newly arrived women had entered the savings group and requested a loan. After a little while, they understood that she would not be able to repay it.

> The women then had to decide together what to do. And they were divided. Many said: "No, she has to give back the money and leave because she has stolen." One of them, Tina, stood up and said: "But if we don't let her remain in the group, and we don't agree to let her repay a little at a time, how will she understand that the measure of her life is not money? And how will she learn to use money well?" There are groups that have failed. But thanks to Rose's help, and to their meetings, the women remain together. This is possible

only because they have understood that there is something here for them.

Tina is the little lively woman with dyed-blonde hair and an Atalanta shirt who was dancing at Kireka. Marco Trevisan, oversees the distance support for different AVSI projects. ("At Luzira, for example, we work with a group that helps the children of those in jail. It is a very poor area, but helping a child to go to school while dad or mom is in jail is a huge support. Sometimes we propose small activities for when the prisoners come out of jail.") He recalls a fact about Tina: "She is very smart: she took out a loan, bought a secondhand motorcycle, and rented it to someone who drives a *boda*, the motor-taxis that jet around all over here." She earns 10,000 shekels a day. "Seventy thousand a week: it is now a small business. She has put some away, and little by little she has bought other motorcycles and now takes in more than a million a month." That is, about $270 a month, enough to live on. "It does not always work so well. Sometimes the loans disappear; there are some who do not pay it back, with the related messes that causes. Or the husbands see the women with money, and they want it. And then another mess, and we start again from the beginning." But Trevisan laughs while he tells the story.

It is quite true: they are not saints. But it is also true that there is something out of the ordinary here. Something "inexplicable," as Repossi said. Otherwise, other facts would not have happened, facts that are disarming in their simplicity.

In August 2005, New Orleans was shocked by Hurricane Katrina: 1,836 dead, 705 missing, $150 billion in damage. When the news arrived, the women from the Meeting Point were shaken up. They went to Rose and asked if they could do something: "We have to help them. We can welcome the Americans in our houses." There were 13,000 kilometers between them, but the women felt the tragedy. When Rose suggested that they say a prayer and observe a minute of silence, one of the women responded more or less like this: "Okay, but we don't want someone just to pray for our children when we die and that's it: we want someone to take care of them. You didn't just pray when you wanted to help us: you shared everything with us." They wanted to do the same. And it didn't take long to find the way: they divided up into groups and decided that a portion of their earnings for the next month would be put aside.

In the end, breaking rocks, they collected two million shekels—at that time more or less $900—to give to the families of the victims. Rose brought it to the American embassy. You can just imagine the face of the person who received the money. A US official asked to meet the women, and a few journalists also came. Some were moved; others were upset: "This is not right: we Americans should be helping you, not the other way around." And another woman there ("she weighed more or less 40 kilograms," Rose recalls) got up and said something that many of the women say, after all those years journeying together: "The heart of man does not have color or race. It is international. It is equal everywhere. It is moved anywhere. We want to share the love that we have received."

Rose says that adding "International" to the name of Meeting Point in some way came from there. But above all, when she recalls this fact, she adds another that concerns her. "At a certain point I realized that they had done all this, and I had not thought to give something of mine! What cracked open my heart was a beggar who came to me with a sack of coins: 'I also want to help the life of someone, I want some child who ended up on the street in New Orleans to be able to buy a sandwich.' It destroyed me. But it this is how it is: when one discovers himself, his heart becomes true."

Five of them, on May 15, 2008, would get up in their colorful dresses with their songs of gratitude on the stage of the New York Women's Foundation, a large American organization for the promotion of women: they were among the recipients at the Celebrating Women Breakfast, together with Christiane Amanpour from CNN and Marie C. Wilson from the White House Project. It will be Teddy, dressed very elegantly in red, who gives thanks, in front of a crowd where some of the most powerful women in America are seated: "Until recently, in Africa, we were all connected to someone: the family, the tribe. You felt important because you belonged to someone. But when you belong, you discover that everything and every person belongs to you. Even the people of New Orleans belong to you, because we belong to someone. We love them, because someone has loved us. And for this reason, we also love you."

In 2009, the story would be repeated. News of the earthquake in L'Aquila, Italy came to Kampala: houses destroyed, 309 dead. The reaction of the women was identical: "We have to help them." With an added motive: "They are Italian; they are the ones who help our children. It is Father Giussani's tribe!" Exactly. Someone asks how long it would take to get to L'Aquila on the bus, to help dig among the rubble: "The Italians are good at doing everything, but no one breaks rocks like we do." They break rocks for two months in their quarry, in groups, just like for Katrina, collecting 1,000 Euros that will end up with the families from Abruzzo through AVSI. At a meeting in Italy, sometime later, they will ask Agnes why the women were moved like that. She answers, "Those people have the same value as us. We felt that we had to unite ourselves to their pain." Then would come the collection for Ukraine, which the Pope's newspaper, *L'Osservatore Romano*, would write about.

It is not easy to keep up with these women. Evening comes and you are dead tired, even if you were only there to watch. They live like this, always. "Look, we waste a ton of energy talking about things," says Rose while the Toyota goes toward Mbuya. "But this is because we haven't understood. We know how to write words, how to form them, but they are not flesh of our flesh. Instead, the Word became flesh." A long silence. "You look at someone like Ketty and say: 'How is she able to be happy? They have tortured and raped her, forced her to harm others, to eat human flesh. . . . How is she still standing?'" Again, a short silence. And then: "But if she is still standing, why not me?"

8

The Method

THERE IS A precise method in all that we have seen. Not a set of user instructions, not a manual, but some key concepts and a way of acting.

To go to the heart of certain key words, on another occasion Rose was called upon to talk about her experience. It was at the 50th International Eucharistic Congress in Dublin on June 15, 2012.

It was an important event for the Church, celebrating fifty years since the Second Vatican Council. In front of cardinals, bishops, and prelates from thirty-one countries and a few thousand of the faithful, Rose said:

> To work and to help others for me means to encourage the emergence of the greatest possible clarity of the value of the person and to offer a precise, specific friendship to which the person can belong. Because the I of the person who belongs becomes a protagonist, begins to have a face, gains a unifying awareness, that unites the self to reality; and reality becomes yours not because you are the one who makes it, but because you discover that you are part of a Design that is not yours, on which you depend. It is the offer of a relationship, a home where each person can discover that he is someone; that he has a value that is not affected or destroyed by his fragility or his sin.

She continued:

> Meeting Point International is a project that goes beyond projects: it lives from the adventure of educating man's heart, of educating the heart to remain in its original position. We form families and communities, that is, places where each person can easily belong.

> ...These families become structures that carry value and meaning in which each child can grow, can develop, and discover his I. We use music, hikes in beautiful places—like valleys and hills, rivers and lakes (for example, the Nile, Lake Victoria, vistas where we can see the sunset)—and traditional dances from the whole world. We have also introduced European songs like Italian Alpine songs and a few Irish, Spanish, and Brazilian songs. Many of these songs were born in difficult moments like wars or other problems, and they speak about love, loneliness, death. But they all show that man has been made for something greater, for an Ideal.

All the work of Meeting Point International serves the person, the I. And community, belonging, is the place that fosters this dynamic. An old African proverb—which Pope Francis also quotes—reminds us that "it takes a village to raise a child": alone we cannot become human. It is true that a village—a community that is truly cohesive, real, and loyal—is born only from men and women who have become fully aware of themselves.

For Rose, everything begins from there, from the awareness of the self and of its destiny, of "something greater, an Ideal" of which man is made and for which man is made: it is Rose's own story that made this clear for her. And everything must point to the generation of a subject that is free, autonomous.

"The Christian proposal always becomes flesh in a witness," observes Julián Carrón, speaking about Rose. "This is the first, fundamental thing. But it is not enough. Because, as Father Giussani says, 'the encounter with a master, with a witness, awakens and fosters the religious sense of man. *But humanity learns by reflecting on itself and its own experience.*' Not even the encounter with a witness can substitute for the personal work of reason. If this awareness is lacking, the subject cannot be generated. The master and the witness 'can make the perception of self, this self-awareness, quicker and much more immediate; *but* the perception of self, one's own act, is irreplaceable.' If we do not get to this point, the person does not grow."

To the prelates in Dublin, Rose used more or less the same words that she had spoken to the pilgrims two years earlier before they left for the Macerata-Loreto pilgrimage:

> I fell into a crisis because I thought that everything depended on me. Now, instead, I have a new awareness of myself and of reality. The poor, the sick, the children . . . what I give them does not impede their destiny, but introduces them to a greater desire, to a new awareness. Medication, food, etc. are the instruments with which I say to them: "You are greater than this, you are greater

than you can imagine, and you yourself are responsible." All the other help I offer is meant to introduce them to Something greater than me, that I do not possess, but that we can recognize together.

The I and God—and a companionship that renders that God approachable, present for you. It is the key for deciphering the life of the women, the schools, the Meeting Point. And it is the key that Rose offers to the public when, at the Meeting of Rimini in 2007, she shows photos to help others *see* her world, the reality that she recounts.

Images pass by of the offices, of T-shirt production, of health education, of women dancing ("We use dance and African music as a cure for depression, because we want to understand and to learn what tradition is: when an African drum sounds, if one is depressed, you see that she begins to move her head, move her feet . . . in a moment she is hooked"). There are images of people watching the sunset: "I saw Italians stop to look at a sunset or a flower, and I said to myself: 'They are crazy.' One day I stopped and looked: it was beautiful. So now with my patients and with the young people, my orphans, we go to the lakes, to the rivers, to the flowers. When I pay for medications, I manage to save something to help them see what someone helped me see, that by looking at beautiful things, people can appreciate their own life. It is something that nobody does, but it works, because it helps one understand the great value of the person."

Then there are the photos of a hike: "Imagine an African woman who says to her husband: 'You stay at home; I have to go on a hike. You look after the children. I am heading out at six in the morning and I will return at six this evening.' But my patients do it, and the husband stays there, and he is also happy when his wife returns."

Other slides: women playing soccer. "One of the women says: 'I am going to play soccer, you take the children,' and the husband follows her with a child on his shoulders, to watch where she is going. And when he finds her playing, he ends up cheering for his wife; he gets mad if he sees his wife lose the ball. Later, he teaches her how to play. One day we were playing close to the police station, and everyone came out to see this game of women. They came to ask us: 'Can our wives join your team?' So, we have included their wives." It seems like nothing, but here are more elements of reflection on the emancipation of women and the equality of the sexes.

Rose speaks about education in hospitality and microcredit. "We give this little loan, and we depend on the capacity of each person to do business, because in this way one feels responsible for her family, even for the families of others." But in the end, she sums up the richness of the photos she has shown in this way: "All this—the projects, the food, all these things—we use as an instrument to say to people: 'You are great, you are greater than you can imagine, you are responsible.' And the projects that we do are like offering a shoulder so that the others can be supported, so that they can take responsibility. We do not say: 'You are nothing, I will feed you, I will give you everything.'"

It is the opposite of welfare dependency: it is a path to help *the person* grow and to help all her potential come out. You see it here in Kampala, where you see how the world that was photographed fifteen years ago has grown.

"The fact is that Rose has total dedication and affection for these people," observes Davide Prosperi. "The women, the children.... She helps them to grow so that they can find their path. She is totally at the service of someone whom she does not consider her property, but rather considers as sacred. Allow me the comparison, but it is a little like Our Lady in front of the baby Jesus: at a certain point Jesus becomes big, and Our Lady has to let him go. Moreover, she has to begin to follow him herself. That is how Rose is there, with this attitude."

One of those slides documented a breakthrough for the Meeting Point. "You know when you understand that something important has happened?" says Clara Broggi. It was a visit of the Italian ambassador to the slum in Kireka. The women, as usual, danced and sang to welcome the ambassador. "But that time each of them introduced herself with a photo of herself," recalls Broggi:

> They danced with the photo in their hand. Rose did not know about it; it was their initiative. And it was something from another world, because these women used to hide themselves at the beginning: they did not speak, they did not say anything to anyone. Or, you spoke with them and they had their head down, or their hands in front of their face. They never raised their eyes. They felt like nothing from a human point of view. They had been thrown out by their families, pushed away. There, for the first time, they said: "We are here, we have a face." I thought: "Wow, what is happening?" That for me was the symbol of their freedom. And of belonging. Both together.

Rose remembers it well: "It was a way of saying to the ambassador: 'Don't worry that we are sick, that we are poor. We are richer than everyone, because we have found ourselves. That is why we dance.'"

Ilaria Schnyder von Wartensee is a Swiss researcher who has worked at length on Meeting Point International for the Kellogg Institute for International Studies of the University of Notre Dame in Indiana. She lived in Kampala for six months and conducted dozens of interviews and focus groups. And she has written a pair of scientific publications that study the method and the reproducibility of Rose's method in other contexts.

One of the articles is "The role of personal identity in human development," published together with Elizabeth Hlabse, Gabriella Berloffa, and Giuseppe Folloni which appeared in *The European Journal of Development Research*.[15] The stated aim was "to describe through a qualitative analysis how personal identity, the awareness of value of the individual, fosters the capacity for action and is at the heart of the process of development."

The references to the literature on the topic include citations from the Nobel Prize winner Amartya Sen and from like Charles Taylor (one of the most important contemporary philosophers) and Paul Farmer (the celebrated anthropologist from Harvard), which seem tailor-made for what is seen in Kireka and Naguru. "There is an element of mystery, of openness and trust in the accompaniment toward development," writes Farmer. "The one who accompanies says: 'I will come with you and I will help you on your journey. . . . I will share your destiny for a while. And with this "while" I am not speaking about something brief.'" Accompaniment indicates remaining attached to a goal until it is completed, and not for the one who accompanies, but for the one who is accompanied." It is exactly what we see in the slums of Kampala.

So many stories of the women are already familiar. Gestures, songs, moments of life. The events of Katrina and L'Aquila. But, from there, Schnyder distills the foundations of the method with which Rose helps the women to gain the awareness of their value. "Her attention to the person," first of all, "fosters a context in which the women can begin to conceive the objectives of their development." Then, there is "mutuality": "Busingye is open to grow and learn together with the women. . . . One of them describes it like this: 'Rose is not in front of us or behind us. She is together with us. She is not the leader. She is with us, and we learn together.'" In the end, "openness to their freedom" exploded when the women began to rediscover their value, to the point that they began to take their medications again. But all this happens because of a constant closeness, an "accompaniment" as the researcher calls it, that lasts in many cases for years (the "journey" that Farmer spoke of).

Schnyder looks again at that song that is so amazing for those who find themselves at Meeting Point for the first time, "When I met Rose": "It is a practice through which the women introduce themselves again, having grown in awareness," but it is also "the instrument through which they describe their experience of sharing in terms of 'belonging.'" In other words, belonging is the factor that, "Busingye explains . . . gives stability and certainty to all the aspects of life."

The Kellogg Institute's research goes to the root, to the origin of this scientifically demonstrated method: "Busingye attributes her work with the women to her religious conviction. For her, faith is a fundamental motivation: she considers her experience of faith as something tightly linked to the awareness of the self, to her own identity, to her own desires; and this is one of the deepest reasons why she continually invites the women to think about the meaning of their life."

Faith. The I and God, again. We return to Father Giussani and to the perception of a God who is present, touchable. "Flesh of my flesh," as stated on that page that ended up in the hands of a young girl from Kampala so many years ago.

In the speech at Macerata, there is a synthesis of this origin. "My work was born from my belonging to a specific place. My work is not an addition to my vocation as a Memor Domini, but the means by which I am affectively fulfilled. What I can give to others is this overabundance of my relationship with Christ within the house; what I give to others is the flourishing of my vocation, the fruit of this fullness of belonging to Christ in a precise place, the discovery of a paternity-in-action within the events of my day, of my existence. From this fact—that is, from faith—I have seen the event of a changed people."

This is why Carrón, speaking of what happened in Kampala, underlines one thing: "There we see that something happens when Christianity is discovered as the answer to the questions of life. Better, to the urgency of living. It is what Father Giussani called 'the totalizing character of faith,' the hold that it has on the whole person and the pertinence it has to all the needs of life: because life is saved as a whole, not in pieces."

If we set out from here, we understand better the insistence with which Rose returns to "her" key words. Belonging, as we have seen. Companionship. And feeling moved. For her it is not a sentimental question, a simple emotional reaction in front of misery or suffering: it is a factor of knowledge; it is the sign that you are truly aware of yourself and thus in relationship with reality.

If you are made by God now, if what you have in front of you—nature, things, the other—is made by God now, how can you not be moved?

"You begin to work because you are moved: if you are moved, you are put in motion, you move," says Rose. "Without feeling moved, things remain sterile, they do not last. Even your commitment sooner or later tires you out. Instead, feeling moved is born from the discovery that you are there and that you do not make yourself. And this emotion throws you into reality without fear even of the errors you will make, of your falls . . . of everything. It is like a child with his father: he feels the hand of his father and isn't afraid of making a mistake, of doing something stupid. He is moved because his father is there. And it is the same for us: your Father is generating you now. Feeling moved is born from this."

Everything around here is based on that. The passionate force and the inexplicable happiness of the women—women who are literally reborn. Beauty breaks out where you least expect it. Even in the profound harmony that you see among some of the protagonists, without which it would be impossible for things to flow as they do. They have very different stories, characters, and temperaments that are difficult to hold together. But each in her own way, her own way of being, sees the depth of reality in the same way. She looks at the same thing, the same origin.

Repossi is also a Memor Domini. Before coming to Africa, he was in the Holy Land for a long time working for AVSI. But it is interesting to hear him talk about his "job interview" with Rose. "We had this lunch at a restaurant in Milan. I asked her: 'What do you need? Someone to run things, sure, but anybody can do that.' And she told me: 'I need someone who lives silence.' A bit peculiar as a job description, but it didn't seem strange to me [he laughs]. I asked her what she meant. And she: 'I need someone who lives his vocation and helps me in this thing. Because within the vocation, when one truly lives it, everything flourishes. Projects, things . . . everything.'"

When he landed in Kampala, he learned something else very quickly:

> The first day at work, Rose brought me into the office and introduced me to everyone. And I began to meet the staff. Two o'clock came, and she called me from Kireka where she had gone out to see the women: "Come to lunch." I had just started a meeting. "Tell her I'm not coming." She called another two times. The third time, I gave in: "Did you make something for me as well? Then I am coming." I took a *boda* and went to her. I thought about telling her:

look, there are office hours, and I have to be there first to give an example. But then the lunch began. And when you talk with her, Jesus is always there in the middle. Not because he is added on: he is so a part of her, that she returns to him in everything. Even if she does not name him. I understood then that that was not a break from work, but rather a chance to take up again the *why* of our work.

Starting that day, lunch together became a rule. "Why does she do it like that? Because when she would return from Father Giussani, he would tell her: 'Go and start a Memores Domini house.' And she always returns home, even for lunch. Because she needs to return to the place that gives her breath, motivation. And with me she is doing the same thing." It is thanks to this that Repossi says that he understands a couple of fundamental things: "I am not here to help an organization, Meeting Point International: the organization is not the walls. I help a person. And Meeting Point, in the end, is not a place that we thought up to help the poor: it exists only in order to share a life, the meaning of life."

There is a final important word that helps us grasp the method that we see at work in these slums of Kampala: *charity*. We need to clear out the reduced image of this word. It is not almsgiving, not even in the worst sense of the rich who give something to the poor to clear their conscience, reiterating their superiority without getting involved, without "touching the hand of the poor man," as the Pope suggests. It is not philanthropy, the massive and well-structured assistance of the "rich world" in these parts, in order to sustain good causes and projects. Nor is it generosity, however priceless, with which many, many volunteers commit to doing good, spending hours, days, entire parts of their lives, helping their neighbor.

In Rose's vision, charity is something more. It is a strange weaving of the divine and the human, of the very nature of God and the misery of man. In an interview for *Soul*, the broadcast of Monica Mondo on TV2000 (the Italian bishops' TV station), on August 31, 2015, Rose cited Benedict XVI and his encyclical *Deus caritas est*: "I understand that he is my friend because there is a part in the encyclical where he describes God and the love of God toward man as 'a divine madness.' The idea that God is madly in love with you: for love of you, God came out of himself to save us, he came, he said 'I am going there....' It is exactly the same thing that Father Giussani told me."

She would explain it much better three years later, in Rimini: "Father Giussani revealed to me that God made for me more than was necessary: He gave himself to me, a total gift of himself. For me, charity, in its nature, is this: God who goes out of himself, like a divine madness. You act in a certain way because within your humanity there is this origin that vibrates in your guts. If this charity is not present in a given moment, none of us here present, or outside of here, can exist: He gave himself to us so that we would be happy, fulfilled." For this reason, again: "My work is to bring to light the value of the individual."

"From what I know of her, it seems to me that her main concern is not first of all 'to do a charitable work,' but to deepen the certainty that all that we do, live, think, feel, is for the glory of Christ," observes Prosperi. "And for her, to live this certainty means to communicate to everyone that we are wanted, loved, esteemed by him. At its root, the true charity that does all these works is to help others feel the love of Christ for the people she encounters and who are with her."

Father Giussani gave a synthetic definition of charity: "The gift of a self that is moved." You see Rose, and you see this charity. And you see how this way of understanding the self and the other generates a sharp intelligence, one that is able to read reality with a surprising depth.

"Rose is capable of unique judgments: of a novelty, of an intelligence that is disorienting, always," says Mónica Fontana Abad, a Memor Domini from Spain and a professor of research methods in the social sciences at the Complutense University in Madrid, where she returned in the summer of 2021 after three years in Uganda. "She is not a cultured person, someone about whom you say, 'she is brilliant from an intellectual point of view.' But she has the intelligence of faith."

This intelligence allows her to make judgments that are very clear, for example, about contemporary society: "It is as if we lived in a civilization that is about to end, because a civilization develops only in the measure it fosters the coming to light and the clarifying of the value of the individual. And today we are going a little bit at a time toward a condition in which man no longer knows who he is. He does not know the meaning of the small things or the great things that happen around him. It is a moment when the identity of the I is put in crisis, every day." Or, about Africa: "The hope of Africa is the same hope that the whole world needs: that there be a man who knows who he is; not only who he is, but whose he is." And then about AIDS, development, war. . . .

The point that according to her has the greatest urgency—that encapsulates everything else—is education. "Our work, in the end, is based on educating the person, because education is the privileged instrument for discovering ourselves."

9

One by One

SHE REMEMBERS the drawing well, even if she does not know where it ended up. A motorcycle. A really big helmet. And a house in the background: tall, solid, like nothing you'd see in the slum. "It was made by a boy who had been kidnapped by rebels and had lived in the forest for a little while," recalls Rose. "One day he entered my office and asked me: 'Rose, help me with the registration fees. I want to go to school and become a soldier. That way I can kill the rebels and get revenge for the death of my parents.'" She thought about it for a few seconds, in silence. "But I decided to bet on his heart. He had already seen too many ugly things: how could he change if he did not encounter something else?" She helped him. Two years later, the same small kid entered through the same door. "He had a luminous face and that picture in his hand. I asked him: 'Why the motorcycle and the helmet?' And he: 'The motorcycle is for you, because I know that you like to go downtown and this way you can do it whenever you want. But the helmet, because here everyone drives crazy, and I love you.' And the house? 'It is for kids like me. We have to welcome more of them. You changed my life, and I want that to happen for many others.' I didn't know it, but that was a prophecy."

She is not exaggerating: that drawing became true. Stone by stone—"brick by brick," as the children's song that is often sung in these parts says—a school was born in the slum. In fact, two schools: one primary and one high school. Plus, a formation center for teachers.

On the streets of Kampala, you see a lot of posters for schools and colleges. It is a profitable business, in a country where half of the 48 million inhabitants are under sixteen years of age: take away those who don't go to school, and there remains at least 20 million young people as the potential clientele for a ton of private schools. The structures are sometimes (not always) better than those of the state schools, where 80-90 children crowd into crumbled and crumbling classrooms in two or three shifts. But the imprint is the same, the old-style Anglo-Saxon establishment: hours of study by memory, multiple choice tests, repetition. Sometimes, beatings: they think that those educate better.

Here, the story is different. And it is born from a "no": the no that the women said to Rose one day in 2006. The episode is described in the exhibit catalogue of the Meeting of Rimini, but in the preparatory interviews for the exhibit, more came out.

That morning, Rose introduced herself at an assembly of Meeting Point in Kireka and threw out the idea that she had taken for granted: "Our sick people are spread out over kilometers, between hospitals and doctors' offices in the area. We need a place where we can gather everyone together, so it is easier to take care of them. We should build a hospital." Silence.

Agnes explained the reason for the silence. For a while the women had been talking among themselves about another problem that they had in common. "So many of our kids went to school, but they were not doing well. They were not bad schools, but the fact is that they were our children, and people always said: 'These kids are sick, they come from families with HIV.'"

One day, one of the children of the slum had fought with a teacher and had been expelled from school. "I went quickly to see, and it came out that he hadn't done his homework. That kid lived a very tough life: his parents were gone, and he had to take care of his younger siblings. But that morning, when the teacher discovered that the boy hadn't studied, the teacher provoked him: 'We are tired of these Kony.' He referred the head of the rebels, associating the boy with them only because he is Acholi. But the boy had been kidnapped by the rebels during the war; he still has a bullet in his leg. To be treated in that way reminded him of his years in the forest: that was why he started to argue with the teacher."

Another time, in another school, one of them didn't return to class right away after a break. "He was out playing," says Teddy, "and a teacher got upset: 'Look at you, you are an idiot: you throw away your time and you don't even know that your mother is dying.' The boy returned home very sad, and the next day he didn't want to go to school anymore. I can tell you so many other facts like this." Facts that told the women one thing, very clearly: "Those schools did not look at our children like human beings. We wanted places that helped them to recognize their value. Rose taught us in this way: even if you are sick, if you are poor, even if your house is a mess. She does not judge this. She comes and hugs you."

For this reason, in front of Rose's proposal, after a few moments of silence, the women answered decisively: "No, not a hospital. We want a school."

The discussion was intense and went on for a while. "Rose asked us: 'And the teachers? Where will we get them from?' And we: "We will educate the teachers with the same system you used with us; then they will be able to take care of our children.'" She insisted: "But I am a nurse: I don't know anything about education. Listen to me, we need to build a hospital." It was then that one of the women got up and said: "You know, Rose, if you build a school, this school will educate doctors, politicians, lawyers, engineers. In the end, it will be more useful than the hospital that you are thinking about."

Rose came back a few days later with another argument: "Look, if we build a hospital, we can start from something small. But a school needs big spaces, classrooms....We don't have money." And there she found herself again in front of another response that she did not expect. "We have talked about it among ourselves and have already decided," said Agnes. "Rose, we will start making necklaces: you find us a place to sell them, and we will build a school with the money we get from them."

The necklaces were the next way Rose's women began to earn something: fake stones, made of colored papier-mâché, bright and beautiful colors. They taught each other the technique. They made them at home, often at night, and later sold them. Precious jewels, if you stop to think where they came from. But costume jewelry costs little at the market: they would need tens of thousands of them. "At that point, Rose challenged us: 'Okay, let's see if you are able.' When she left, we continued the meeting: 'We have to show her that we have understood our value and are capable of doing it. Let's work together, hand in hand, here at Meeting Point.'"

This is how Agnes says it: "Hand in hand." A chain that expands, one woman at a time. It overcomes family barriers, breaks down tribal borders, and becomes very powerful. "Teddy and I spent days going from house to house to be sure that everyone was working, to check the quality of the necklaces: they had to be beautiful. Then Rose came to us one day saying: 'I spoke with our friends from AVSI. We can send them to Italy.'"

The different accounts about the number of necklaces sold—between missionary markets, the Meeting of Rimini, and other meetings—vary: there are some who count 32,000, others up to 48,000. But with that money the women bought sacks of cement, bricks, sand. They brought them to a property found by Teddy's husband, who was a kind of village chief. And they began to construct the first building.

"I was in the car one winter evening, on the industrial outskirts of Milan, and the phone rings" remembers Giampaolo Silvestri, the general secretary of AVSI. "It was Rose: 'Look, we bought a property for the school. The chief here told me that we can do it, and we are doing it, even if the documents are not all together yet. What do you think?' And I: 'Rose, what do you want to do? Let's give it a try.'"

"I don't know if Rose still had the idea about the hospital, because she didn't speak about it anymore," laughed Agnes. "But all this came out because we had discovered ourselves, who we are. We cannot be reduced to our sickness. We are normal people, and we are capable of building a school."

There was not much need to discuss the name of the school. "Rose proposed that we name it after Luigi Giussani," says Teddy. "And the women agreed right away. Because we knew all that she had said to educate us came from him. Giussani was already in our hearts, even without ever having seen him. Every time we asked Rose about her life, she responded: 'My life is this way thanks to him.' That name for us was a home."

Today there are two signs with that name: when the number of students increased, a high school was formed from the primary school, which had to move to another part of the slum. And our visit today begins at Luigi Giussani High School. You go through the gate, onto the dirt road that goes up from Kireka Banda towards Kamuli, passing through the usual chaos. And you find yourself suddenly in another world, a world of order and cleanliness. A small building with three floors, with uniform rows of balconies and gray railings, in contrast to the orange-yellow paint of the walls. Right next to this building, without any space in between, there is another building, with a uniform façade broken by vertical windows and a large entrance door, the same color somewhere between orange and yellow. It was built later, when money came in from AVSI and other donors. It has another floor with a glass window. It overlooks hedges, flower beds, and a row of palms trees that line the little internal gravel road. The rocks come from the quarry where the women work. But the rest, ultimately, comes from there. The bricks, the palm trees, the hedges. The steps where the kids are studying in groups. The soccer field, with goals and nets and the basketball court. The gradient that slopes down leaving space for an orchard. All of this came from the labor of the women and from the doors that they knew how to open.

"We finished the first portion in 2012, the second two years later," recalls the principal. His name is Matteo Severgnini, or just "Seve," forty-one years old from eastern Lombardy, a graduate in philosophy with blond curly hair, a confident character with a sharp intelligence. He arrived here in 2012. Rose needed some help: someone who spoke the same language about education. And Severgnini, a young vice-principal of the Traccia School near Bergamo, from Communion and Liberation and a Memor Domini, was among the first names that came out. "It was an occasion to deepen my vocation," he explains.

Now he is here, in charge of this little city populated by five hundred students, forty-one teachers, and twenty or so employees. There are twelve sections, two for each year of high school. "In Uganda, there are two school cycles: seven years of primary and six of secondary." These are subdivided in two: four years open to everyone and the same for everyone, then two years of specialization—the advanced level—with access only for the best students, which serves as a gateway to university studies. It is a tight funnel, which, coupled with the ruling business model, has an effect on the schools. "You have to perform, to produce graduates," says Severgnini. "The more "division ones" (the highest grade on the exams) you get, the more you attract students, the more money you make." And to arrive at division one, the schools use every means necessary: from corporal to psychological punishments, to the pain that is, many times, the school itself. "In certain boarding schools, the schools that go for the best, they study thirteen hours a day: they make the kids get up at four in the morning and they go to bed at ten in the evening." Here, no. At first, this difference created problems: "Not so many wanted to come here, even from the slums." Why? "One, it was seen as 'the school for the Acholi,' and so only for the kids of Rose's women. Two, because they were children of women with HIV. And three, because we don't beat kids here: and not seeing us use violence, many people said: 'They don't study there.'"

But that is not true. And not only because the results say the opposite (Luigi Giussani is one of the best schools in the country, with seventy percent of graduates admitted to the universities), but also because of how they arrived here: step by step.

"The school was not born automatically: it came out of a desire, from a need to know our own value," continues Severgnini. "We tried to build it keeping this point in mind, always. Everything that you see came from there, and from what was happening among us." For example? The color of the walls. "The kids really like mangos; it is the sweetest fruit, and it is easy to find here. Many of the women make a living by selling them. So we said to ourselves: OK, we will make the school that color." This is why the plaster is painted yellow-orange: the color of the mango.

The inside walls are the same color. In the atrium on the right side, there is a painting towering over the kids who are talking among themselves on a bench. It is *First Steps* by Van Gogh: the mother crouched down to support the child, the father who waits for the little girl with open arms a few meters away. In the middle, the space of autonomy that must be conquered, of an "I" that grows and begins to become herself. She is immersed in the embrace of her parents, and together she begins to go out on her own. Severgnini sees that you stop to look at it: "Even that has a reason." And he tells it: "Before coming here, I went around to a few Ugandan schools to get an idea of how to build it, what to put here. In almost every school there is a 'talking compound,' a space where the kids who mess up are gathered together and where the rules are repeated to them. Fine. But for me, rules have always taken the wind out of kids. Speaking with the principal and other professionals, we said: we did not grow up this way. We became mature within another rule: the rule of relationship, in relation with someone who loves you. And we wanted everything here to speak of that."

When the second building opened in 2014, they asked sixteen-year-old Arnold to give a testimony. "And he, in front of a thousand people, exhorted us like this: 'Luigi Giussani is not a school; it is a home: I run every morning to get here, because I know that there is someone waiting for me.' We looked at each other: no one had ever called the school a 'home.' I for one had never thought of it. This image of running to school because there is someone waiting for you struck us. With the principal, we said: 'It would be beautiful to put up an image that helps us remember this.' And we chose this one." It describes "the educational question" says the director, "to be embraced and welcomed. Van Gogh uses the same color of the sky, which is the dwelling place of God, for the house and the clothes of the parents: everything is blue. Because the home is where you are loved. God, the house, the sky, then the colors. This is basically what Arnold said to us." And the prophecy of that little boy to Rose, years before.

The paintings we see contain "a fact that happened, something concrete: they are our historical memory." Next to *First Steps*, there is the "eco-painting" in earth, grass, sand, and charcoal, made by a kid that depicted the school building. On the back wall, there is an image of Father Giussani. On the left, another Van Gogh, *Almond Blossom*, "which is the idea of Christ incarnate, of a beauty that precedes you. Here—if you place yourself here, in the middle of the entrance—you see three things: our idea of education, the charism from which it was born, and the origin of everything. The three pillars of the school. But we only realized it later: we did not plan it like this." And do the students know it? "No. Or, the ones who ask know. Many left after six years and never asked about it. Many others, instead, have asked, and we explain it to them. The idea is that knowledge always begins with a question' we are not the ones to impose it."

We go up the staircase, outside the building. Our gaze turns to classrooms full of life and red T-shirts. Two kids pass the director coming down the stairs: greetings, jokes, smiles. "Do you know them all?" "All of them, one by one." A few steps later there is a science laboratory, with thirty heads bent over their desks. On the walls here, there are photos in black and white: from Galileo to Einstein, each with a phrase next to it. "They are our friends," explains Severgnini. He shares where they come from as well:

> Four or five years ago, Solange, a student, knocked on my office and started crying. "Seve, I don't know what's wrong, but I am sad. I always feel wrong, in the wrong place, with the wrong people." Here people never talk about depression, but in short, that's what it was. She continued crying and saying, "I am not well." "Is there anyone you can be with that will help you feel better?" "No." "And do you feel this way the whole day?" "Yes." At a certain point she froze and said: "No, there is a moment of the day that is different: it is after dinner, when I escape from the house, and I go out to look at the stars." I stayed silent. I hurriedly looked up a poem by Leopardi, "The Night Song of a Wandering Shepherd in Asia." "Look, here is someone who thinks like you." I read her a few passages. And she brightened up: "But how is this possible? These are my questions. You have to introduce me to him!" I confess that I thought: now she is really going to be depressed. "Look, Solange, this is an Italian poet who died two hundred years ago." And she, instead of reacting badly: "But how is it possible that I feel the same questions as someone from the 1800s?" "Maybe the stars and the moon that you see are the same that he saw, and your heart is identical to his and to mine. Even I have these questions." She gave me a smile and said: "Thank you. Now I have a friend." But she was not talking about me, she was talking about Leopardi."

Severgnini told the story to his colleagues. And from this came the idea of placing photos of these "friends" around. In the library, for example, there are Shakespeare ("There are more things in heaven and earth, Horatio, than are dreamt of in your philosophy.") and Charles Dickens ("What I want is Facts. Teach these boys and girls nothing but Facts: nothing else will ever be of any service to them."); and in the computer lab, Steve Jobs: "The only way to do great work is to love what you do."

In the teacher's lounge there is a phrase hanging up: "Teaching is the adult way of learning." "It is the motto that the teachers chose." And how did you choose it? "We look for three things in our teachers," Severgnini responds. "The first is a mental openness that can understand the difference of this school. It is not easy to come here: some teachers begin and after a week they leave. They say: 'If I cannot use strong measures, the kids will never listen to me.' Those that remain do so because they recognize a different climate. Second, obviously, they have to know the material. Third, the method. We try to understand if the person is able to teach." A few years ago, there was an English teacher, George, who is doing his Masters now. "He told us that after the interview he couldn't sleep: 'If they take all these steps, that means the son of the president is probably at this school.'" They hired him. Two, three weeks, a month, go by, and he realized that not only was there no scion of a VIP, but the majority of the kids came from the slums. "He did not understand. After a few months, he told us: 'At the beginning I thought you all were crazy. But then I understood that for you they are all the children of presidents. And I understood this because I also had the same experience. Here, I feel like the son of a king.'"

From a distance, it may seem sentimental. But it is not. It is just something that goes deeper than where our thoughts usually stop, our "rationality," the habitual measure. In the end, it is the flashpoint of Rose's experience that comes back to the foreground, always and only this: you have a value. You *are* a value. Greater than your schemes and categories.

Another wall, other faces. Four saints this time: Dominic Savio, Agnes, Therese of Lisieux, and Kizito, Uganda's child martyr. They give the names to the houses, the teams into which, in the Anglo-Saxon tradition, the students are divided in order to participate in games and competitions. Four groups that spread across different ages, to create bonds bigger than the classes, the ages, the usual friendships. And the tribes, a factor that must always be kept in mind in these parts. When you ask him if the tribal divisions have a lot of weight, Severgnini is clear: "Yes. Every war in Africa is born and is nourished from there. I see it even among us, in our small way: we need to pay attention to it."

In the beginning, there were 275 kids, almost all Acholi, because Rose's women were for the most part from that tribe and almost all were sponsored from abroad with distance adoptions. Now the circle has expanded among the families and the students. In the school, there are people from thirteen different ethnicities and languages. A nice melting pot, multiplied by the religious factor (among the students, a third are Protestant and five percent are Muslim). "This shared life is good also because we have professors from every tribe." It is another factor to keep in mind, in selecting groups. "At the educational level, it helps to maintain equilibrium: because if problems begin to show up, we Westerners do not always recognize it," adds Severgnini. "I have been here for ten years, and I still struggle to read certain dynamics. I don't see them. Maybe I will never see them. If you do not have someone you trust to advise you, you risk opening up cracks." Subtle—but dangerous—cracks.

On one wall, there is a memory board, a blackboard with pictures of the friends who have passed through here: Julián Carrón; Davide Prosperi, his successor; Jesus Carrascosa (from Spain, a CL leader who has greatly helped the community in Uganda and in the rest of Africa); Francesco Frigerio, an engineer from Treviso and a friend of many and a great help in the construction of the school, who died at age thirty-seven in an accident on the road to Gulu. Many of the sponsors come and meet the children they help from a distance. Then, the photos of students that graduated: all of them, year by year.

But what Severgnini calls "one of the most beautiful places" at the school is in the basement.

> It is a gift that we wanted to give to Rose: a couple of years ago she had downloaded an app that tells you the names of the stars and for weeks she was obsessed. Wherever she went, she looked at the stars and the cell phone: "Look, this is Sirius.... There is Jupiter!" But the other reason is a lesson in itself. We were speaking about space. I was very tired, so I improvised: "Close your eyes and imagine you are flying, and you see the school from above. Then you go up again and you see the neighborhood, you go up and you see your house. And then Kampala, and then Uganda...." I more or less made them go into orbit, but they had never thought of something like that. At a certain point, a young girl, Rachel, says to me: "Seve, stop; my head is spinning; I have to open my eyes."
> "Okay, let's open our eyes. But why is your head spinning?" "Because I don't know where we are going." "That is the point: we are

going into the infinite." And she, I will never forget her face: "And what is the infinite?" To help her understand, I couldn't think of anything except to ask: "Kids, in your opinion is there something of the infinite here among us? Something that is like the universe?" And another young girl, Joan, got up and said: "Yes, my heart. My heart is without an end, like the universe." I was moved. To remember this lesson, we put up this image.

It is a blown-up picture of the Milky Way. Placed in the basement, because "we wanted to make this play between the infinite and the finite: the highest thing is in the most ugly hole of the school."

A nun passes by and introduces herself. "Sister Stella, religion teacher." When she leaves, Severgnini explains that she is the only religious in the school; she came on board eight years ago: "During the trial period, there was a soccer match, professors versus students. I was up in my office: at a certain point I heard shouting, I went down and saw Sister Stella in the goal, with her skirt pinned up like shorts and her veil like a bandana, and she was screaming like a crazy woman. 'Perfect, if we are going to hire a sister, I want her!'" He laughs. "She is great with the students. And I discovered that she was a friend of Father Tiboni; we didn't know it."

There is another painting that says a lot about this school. It is *The Return of the Prodigal Son* by Rembrandt. It is hung in one of the landings of the stairs: it is impossible not to pass by it many times a day. Each time, Severgnini remembers the story that brought it there. "Five years ago, Daniel, one of our students, beat up another student, just outside the school," he recalls.

> Imagine the mess: here where we always say, "Don't hit each other," "the value of the person," etc. I called Rose, and we brought in the family the day after. Daniel and his father introduced themselves. Rose gave Daniel a long tirade: "Respect for the other. . . . Here we love you. . . . How do you allow yourself. . . ?" After a good half hour, little Daniel—who evidently could not take any more—got down on his knees and broke down crying: "I am sorry; I am sorry; I will never do it again." I picked him up and said: "Daniel, let's do this: we will suspend you for one week, so that you can think about what you are going to do, then you return. Now go home with your dad." I looked at Rose and we said to each other, without words: "He's understood." "Yes, I think he understood me." We both returned to our work. I went into my office. After half an hour, the telephone rang: it was the police. "Severgnini, we

have one of your students here." I think: impossible, they are all in school. . . . No, it's Daniel!"

Severgnini jumped in the car, arrived at the police station ("a hut with two benches") and found Daniel there with a woman who was looking at him awry, holding her purse close to her. "He tried to rob me." "No, she is the one who fell on me." They are very tough here on thieves. "Thanks be to God he had on the school uniform; if not, there was a big risk," says Severgnini. The director spoke to the police, and Daniel managed to avoid jail. But the police were inflexible about one thing: "Okay, he can go home, but first we have to punish him." And the director had to try really hard to keep back his tears, while he watched Daniel take ten blows. He took him away in the car, and Daniel fell apart. He could only mumble: "You should not have let me go." "It was heartbreaking," recalls Severgnini.

As soon as they stop at Naguru, Rose's car arrives right behind them. "She gets out and kneels in front of little Daniel, who was staggering. Rose was crying: 'Forgive me, I treated you badly. I reduced you to the mistake you made.' I was crying too, like an idiot. But I can never forget that moment, because, in my opinion, it was the greatest educational scene I have ever seen. You do not educate someone until you can kneel down before the heart of the other. It is the only way to correct truly."

Daniel finished school. The last two years were difficult: "He rebelled; he didn't obey the teachers; every now and then he hit his classmates." He came really close to expulsion. And the one who saved him from the anger of the professors was Sister Stella: "If we say that the kids are more than the mistakes they make, we cannot send him away. I will take care of him from now on; I will be his guardian angel." He took his exams, graduated ("with really high grades, because after all that it turns out he was a genius") and then disappeared. After two months, he came to the director: "They told me that you put up my image in the school." It was *The Prodigal Son.* "And I: 'Well, calm down. Yes, we hung a picture that represents you and Sister Stella.' 'Why Sister Stella?' He didn't know anything about her involvement. I told him. He wanted to see the painting." And, in front of Rembrandt, tough Daniel started to cry: "You are the only friends I have had in my life." He went away, and they no longer saw him here. But who knows what remained inside him.

You listen, and the words of Agnes and Teddy come to your mind, a profound wisdom that always boils down to this: "We need to understand who we are, and we need to be educated in order to do it, because it doesn't come out of nowhere. This is the reason why we have the schools. Even if you get a PhD, in the end you need this awareness of your value. And if while you were studying, they didn't teach it to you, then what use is your PhD? Are you somehow different from the person who stopped at elementary school? We are all equal. There are a bunch of people who have everything, money, a good life, a beautiful house, living in a skyscraper, but they are not happy. Because they don't know who they are."

Here in Uganda, the results of the State Exams are a kind of national ceremony. Sometimes they announce the results on the radio. "The first time that our candidates took the exams, we were very happy," says Teddy. "The results arrived during one of our meetings: as soon as we found out, we began to run and jump. We went to the school, bringing along our drums, because we were so happy. We began to sing and play outside the gate. The reaction of some of the teachers was . . . well, you know, here it is like our home: there was no need to tell them that we were there. They were happy, like us. They joined us with all the students outside the classrooms. Seve brought something to eat, and we danced and danced. . . ."

Two years later, the results were not as good. But the reaction, in some ways, was even more interesting. "We said to ourselves: let us have a party all the same," Agnes says. "We are parents; we know our children. They are all different: some are a bit behind; some are more advanced. But they all passed. And we, therefore, are happy. Our kids are not their grades: they are human beings, with their value and their dignity. And nothing can reduce them." Agnes did not study as a child. Many of Rose's women learned to read and write only at Meeting Point. They know nothing about educational theory and pedagogy. But the essential, yes, that they know very well: "The school is like life: sometimes you are down, but that shouldn't stop you. The next time it will go better; you can't let up. This is the education that Rose gave us: you are not reduced to what happens to you, because the thing that truly counts is the discovery of yourself."

It is the same vision that animates the other Luigi Giussani, the primary school. A twin school, planted in the heart of the slum. Even the principal, in some ways, looks like the director of the other school. A young guy from Bergamo, he is a great friend of Severgnini, who invited him to come here when he understood that the work was too much for one person alone. His name is Andrea Nembrini; he too is a Memor Domini, and he has a similar path: Catholic University of Milan, the vocation to teach. He is the child of an artist: his father, Franco, is famous for his books and TV programs on education, as well as for being a brilliant student of Dante.

Now he is walking on the place "where everything began, where the village chief said to the women: 'Okay, you can use this area.'" It was a rugged, barren field—all rocks, brambles, with cows passing through. Now it is a well-kept meadow with a long hedge on one side and the first building put up fifteen years ago, which today functions as the kindergarten and kitchen. There is a soccer field with bleachers where the young ones climb around during recreation in their neat uniforms: blue T-shirt and shorts for the boys, checked dress and white socks for the girls, a red sweater for everyone when needed.

Close by is the school itself: "put up in installments, one piece at a time," says Nembrini, who, when he arrived in Uganda in 2016, found himself "more a foreman than an educator." Here there was a strip of land to be levelled, next to a fence that kept the goats away from the rainwater tank, "and here there was an orchard belonging to one of the women, who did not take it well." The building has two floors: it houses seven grade levels and 520 students, including those in kindergarten, and a staff of eighteen teachers. On the ground floor, there are offices; on the upper floor are the classrooms and a balcony from which you can see the intricate weaving of alleys and sheet roofs of the slum all around. Another world, just a wall away. "It took a while to realize what a difference it makes for them to arrive each morning from there and enter here."

The classrooms are bursting: between 50 and 65 students in each, "but it is a third the size of the standard schools of the country." In one, with the windows facing the slum, there is a group that is a little smaller: twenty or so kids, of all ages. "It is a post-Covid experiment," explains Nembrini. "Cross cutting, lessons mixed by age for those who are re-entering school with more problems: after two years at home, without distance learning, there are huge differences. And there are those who come from other schools without even knowing how to write. Achram, who is nine years old, is seated next to Chobe, a tall and athletic adolescent. "We will see how this trimester goes, then we will decide when to bring them back to their class."

Stacked up against a wall there are boxes of books with the government seal. "They had to do for studying at home. The government promised them when the pandemic began, but they only just arrived," Nembrini smiles. The benches are almost new: a gift from a donor, like so much here. Many students have sponsors who support them from a distance, from Italy and other places. Because solidarity expands by contagion. "There is our gymnastics teacher, Dixon, who every now and then goes to teach lessons in the slums," recounts Nembrini. "One day he came in and said: 'Outside there is a young kid named Leyton. I would like to pay the fee for him to come to school.' And I: 'Why?' 'You know, Andrea, I was helped by Meeting Point as a little kid. I am what I am because from the other part of the world someone who didn't even know me loved me and bet on me. Because of what I received, I also want to give.'" After two years, Leyton returned to his village, in the North. "But Dixon continues to pay for his studies."

Nembrini says that it was not easy to adapt. It is never easy to enter into another world or another's skin. Culture, mentality, ways of doing things . . . everything is different. "And there remains a distance in the way they look at you. It was hard for me, at the beginning: also because it is something that repeats when new students arrive. But the difference is not the decisive thing. In fact, sometimes it makes everything even more beautiful." In what sense? "Because you realize that the difference is not determinative: the heart is the heart, wherever you are." The same desires, the same needs. "There is no difference that can distance you ultimately from the other. Many times, you speak with parents and ask yourself: are we understanding each other? And you see that yes, you are, and it is a joy. Sometimes it seems like the true work that we are doing here, in the end, is the attempt to eliminate these distances. Betting everything on those human essentials: love, patience, time that does not belong to you."

Nembrini calls its "a permanent destabilization: I find myself moved, always. And I learn, continually." It happened right away, from the first impact. "When I arrived, it seemed that nothing was working. At the kindergarten, for example, there were no toys. I went around Kampala like an idiot to look for beautiful toys. I found them; we bought them, and we would teach the teachers how to use them. And, after the first morning, we found them destroyed." He was discouraged and told Rose about it: "How can they do this? They are vandals." And she: "It is clear that you have not yet understood anything. The problem here is not 'rich or poor, black or white.' Teach them that they have value. Here, no one ever says anything about it. If they discover that they have value, you will see that they know even how to value their toys, their teachers, their classmates. . . ." Yes, he still remembers that "displacement." "You have your idea of how things should go, and instead no: the point is not that, but to regain a certainty. You have to take another road. 'You have to take another journey,' Dante wrote. Which maybe passes through Hell and Purgatory...." He says it smiling.

And the families? "Some recognize that what we are trying to do is revolutionary, but interesting. Other have more difficulty." On Saturday, there are meetings with the parents. "This year I have already done four. There wasn't one where a father did not stand up and say: 'Mister principal, this school is beautiful, thank you for what you do. But you have to beat our children; if not, they do not learn. I don't understand why you are all afraid to do it.' Often, though, right afterward, some other parent gets up, who has been in the school a little longer, and replies: 'It is not true. It may seem like physical force works, but it doesn't: after a little while they get used to it, and you don't have any other instruments....' To pass on this idea that we are all educating together is an endless task."

With Covid, Ugandan schools closed for two years. Distance learning was unthinkable. Everyone at home, period. Twenty-four months without lessons, professors, homework. For many of the kids, it meant also doing without the meals that the school guarantees. It is not easy to imagine the drama of an entire generation abandoned to itself for two years: definitely not "value." But the high school teachers found a way to establish a minimum of connection with their students: they went around the slum on motorcycles, bringing notes and homework house to house. Severgnini says that "the reactions of the students went from 'how beautiful to see you' to 'how the heck did you find me here?' They were both surprised and happy." And he laughs. Nothing of the sort had ever been done, and not only in Kampala.

"It is the method of our schools, and we are proud of it," says Agnes. "No one else takes care of our kids like this. So many parents saw what the teachers were doing and asked: can I bring my children to your house? They understood that for us the students have a value. And we want the Luigi Giussani schools to be like *karagali* seeds: they are small, but the tree that is born from them is very big."

10

Freedom

"THIS IS NOT the career I thought I would be doing. I studied something else. But when Rose asked me to come here, I took the invitation very seriously. I thought: 'Well, the women have to face so many challenges: sickness, poverty, family problems.... I would be able to help them be happier.' Instead, working with them is helping me first of all." Clare Adoch looks straight ahead while she speaks. It is not a way to avoid eye contact or my questions as she sits on the bench against the wall at Meeting Point. She is choosing her words with care. She wants them to flower from an experience, despite her youth. She is twenty-six years old, and for five years she has worked here as a social worker, and recently coordinating the team of caseworkers. She explains why the surprising proposal Rose made to her became more valuable: "I see how they live, and I see something that I did not expect: it is very different from my thoughts. I knew so many of them, but to see up close the way they face challenges without feeling reduced to their problems continuously surprises me. And I want to be like them, to live like them, to face challenges like them. With the same awareness. Being with them is a great opportunity for me to grow."

Her mother has the same story: "When Clare arrived in Kampala, she was alone. She did not have an easy life. At a certain point, though, she joined Meeting Point. And I remember those days, because she was always excited and spoke about the women and about what they were doing together: they danced and sang, and she always came home happy." Here they found help: a sponsor for Clare and her two brothers. "They were in primary school; I was able to finish school and go to university." And there she also met CL. "My mother took care of Father Tiboni in 2012 when he was sick. Rose invited her to School of Community,[16] and she began to tell us to go there as well. In the beginning, to tell the truth, it was hard: I didn't understand the book; the words were very difficult for me. But when I arrived at the university the second year, I began to understand: the experiences that we were sharing helped me to live. It is one of the greatest gifts I have had from my relationship with Meeting Point." The greatest for her also is the bond with Rose. "For me she is a friend and a mother, both together. She showed me love and tenderness. But above all, she is the one who I look to constantly, for the way she lives her life."

Clare is one of the many kids who have grown up in Rose's world. There are dozens of who were brought up during these years: children of the women and of the slum, children literally taken from the street. They have studied, they have gone to university, and now they are working. Many of them work here as well, at Meeting Point. You see them busy with administrative paperwork or in the teachers meetings, and the clear impression is of something firm: fresh blossoms on branches of a tree planted in good soil, the kind that lasts.

They are fruits of an investment in education which in these parts is enormous, in every sense. Beyond the two Luigi Giussani schools, there is COWA, which has a different purpose, independent of the schools. It is a vocational training center, a professional school, born in 1998 from the Italian Companionship of Works Association (COWA), supported by AVSI. "They teach courses in agriculture, carpentry, construction, hairdressing. About sixty students," says Repossi, while the Toyota takes the dirt road that leads to the other end of the high school and the navigator all of a sudden starts to speak in Japanese ("We just brought it to the mechanic, and this is the result."). Going past the gate, a large green panorama opens up. Five or six tidy sheds, pieces of land transformed into greenhouses or cultivated as vegetable gardens, small spaces reserved for bananas and mangoes. The sound of chickens comes from the shed.

In front of the main office building, which is long and low, also painted like a mango, is the director. Her name is Chrispine Wanyahoro; she is from Kenya and a Memor Domini. She lives with Rose and has worked here since 2015, when she came because "they needed someone to help them start again." She left a post in a government office in her own country. She says that she came to Kampala having in mind something Father Giussani said, years before: "He was speaking about Uganda: 'The problem in a place is if there is or is not a Father who takes care of it. We think that we come to solve problems. In reality, it is Another who is at work.' So, I left with this provocation: to see how this Father has kept them and me in mind. To work here is a continuation of what I live in the house: it is the continual discovery that first of all I am loved."

This is what makes her welcome the kids. "They are those who do not do well at school or do not have any other path. When their parents bring them to us, they speak about a last chance." It is a condition that many in Uganda face: each year, almost six million young people finish school. Only ten percent continue their studies: for the others, the challenge begins of finding a path. "Many remain without a future. Here we try to give one to them."

The courses last from six months to two years. Under a shed, Goretti, a young woman, is watering a hydroponic microsystem: she says that her dream is "to have my own farm" one day. "Agriculture is the principal sector here, and it offers the greatest opportunity for work." The chickens that we heard before belong to Julian, who is twenty-five years old; he arrived in 2018 to study for two years. Then Covid stopped everything. And COWA made a proposal to him: use the space to start your own micro-farm. A start-up, in short: little in the way of technology, but sufficient to help him learn a trade and pour himself into it. Others will learn to be carpenters, or blacksmiths, or to grow mushrooms: all things they teach here, together with the foundations of work. "A young person who has nothing to do does not know who he is," says Wanyahoro. "But if you put them to work, to take care of things, they see that this piece of reality, thanks to them, changes. And they move, because it interests them."

More or less six hundred people have gone through here during these years. The professional school still has a relationship with a hundred of them. They maintain contact with almost all of those who finish the courses, for at least a couple of years: "We have an office set up to follow them. We call them, we try to understand how it is going, if they have found work. If we can, we help them." Eight out of ten are working after one year. But all have seen something useful for their lives.

Many arrive from hard situations, the director says. There are difficult children: "sometimes you bring them for an internship and the owner calls you to say that they stole something or that they didn't show up." The road is long. "But many of them make a connection, and they return. There is one who disappeared for three years, and then one day we saw him again: 'I am sorry I didn't give notice.' We knew that he had been in prison. But he returned to take up school again, after all that time." She stops. "It is a miracle." Silence again. "The truth is that I look at them and I think: 'And I? If I had not had someone who took care of me, would I be different from them?'"

What they call the "Giussani Family," though, has another child. It was born later, in 2009, but it has the features of an older brother. It is a well-kept structure, full of offices and classrooms that you could find in an Italian university. No children, no high-schoolers: the students going around here are older. It is the Luigi Giussani Institute of Higher Education (LGIHE), a center that organizes formation for teachers and NGO workers. "A place where the vision of Father Giussani is proposed starting from *The Risk of Education*, one of his fundamental works," explained Mauro Giacomazzi, Deputy Principal of the Institute, in a *Traces* article some time ago. "Giovanna Orlando and Clara Broggi, two Memores who live with Rose and who work in Uganda for AVSI, first thought it up. Giovanna died before she could see the work completed."[17]

In the beginning it was started to form our kindergarten and primary school teachers," explains Mónica Fontana Abad, who has worked on the board of the Institute for three years. "But with time we said: why not expand this possibility to others? It is a crucial formation."

Today the center offers "training for school administrators, teachers, social workers, and students," with a focus on one point, underlined in the first paragraph of the program: "Teacher Identity: to help teachers discover themselves and their role in education, to become a point of reference."

In the introduction, there is "Our Theory of Change." Three clear points, made of "if/then" statements: "*If* we gaze upon the person while recognizing his/her value and dignity, *then* we shall be able to foster a sense of belonging that reawakens a self-awareness in front of reality. *If* the person becomes self-aware, *then* everything that he/she encounters becomes meaningful and interesting. *If* the person discovers the meaning of reality, *then* he/she engages with reality and becomes capable of confronting daily life situations with unwavering positivity and openness." Next there is a diagram with four icons and the arrows that connect them: from a gaze to the discovery of the self, to interest in things, to a person who becomes "a protagonist."

The same method is found here as well. The same road that the women of Meeting Point International, the students of the primary and the high school, the kids at COWA all follow. But it happens in a place where this idea of education—better, this experience—has become a subject of study, an occasion for enrichment, a patrimony to share.

Since 2013, the year when it was recognized by the National Council for Higher Education, the Institute entered an international network of a certain caliber. It has relationships with the Universities of Notre Dame (USA) and of Eichstätt (Germany), with the RELI (Regional Education Learning Initiative) of East Africa and the Austrian Development Agency. It publishes scientific research on "Reform of Assessment in Uganda" and on "Critical Thought as the Key to Learning." Beyond the formation in these classrooms, there are conferences and seminars abroad: South Sudan, Kenya, Congo, Mozambique . . . but also Thailand, Myanmar, Palestine. In one way or another, the "LGIHE Method" has touched the lives of over 25,000 people: educators, students, and families.

It is a bet—on the future and on the young. It comes from a broad gaze, oriented toward building a tomorrow for a country that has great need of it (the women and their request come to mind: "With a school we will educate doctors, lawyers, politicians . . ."). But this breadth is not generic: every form of organization, even the most structured—the schools, COWA, the Institute—helps the individual child grow, one by one. On October 8, 2018, to the center's first graduates center (the "pioneers"), Rose said: "This moment is for you, so that you can be true men and women. All that you have acquired here must be a lamp that illuminates all the horizons of your intelligence—not just one plus one, but the totality of your lives."

The totality. When she looks at the young people, Rose does not see only a future, someone to be educated in view of tomorrow: she sees something that is urgent now, a challenge in the present. And she has the same expectation for herself: "So many times it is the kids who educate me."

This is an important moment that helps us understand what happened between the young people who gravitated to Rose and her women. The Meeting of Rimini 2010 was titled "That nature that pushes us to desire great things is the heart." It is a phrase from Father Giussani. The first event, the afternoon of August 22nd, was a testimony: "At the heart of experience: reborn after an encounter." Together with Rose, five dark-skinned kids get up on the stage: Deogracious, Fredy, Caesar, Denis, and George William, who at Baptism chose the name Luigi Giussani.

They all tell their stories. They have three things in common. One: a sharp, heart-breaking pain, lived each in his own way. George's parents were burned alive on a bus set on fire by rebels: "The world at that point took on the character of a total darkness. I thought that I would be next, and I did nothing but look forward to the day of my death." Caesar also lost father and mother in the war: "Life for me was nothing but the desire not to live and to die. Why should I live if there is no way to be happy on this earth?" And the same for Fredy. Deo's mother and five brothers remained alive: "She was not able to pay the school fees for all six of us. So after fourth grade, we all had to begin working in the rock quarries."

The second point in common, though, is that all five of them had an encounter that opened another perspective: Aunt Rose. And her women. "They worked in the quarry, and yet they were singing, dancing, and they were happy," says Caesar. "How is it possible to be happy when you are hungry and sick? I thought they were a bit stupid. Or drunk." And Fredy: "Then someone came to me to talk about Meeting Point, and I said to myself: let's see what this is, let's go listen to what they have to offer me. I went and met Rose. I was expecting to find a boss, a great woman in the office. Instead, I found someone who worked with the other women: she was there, she danced, she was one of them. I asked myself: is this the head of Meeting Point?"

The third fact in common happened in 2007, when Julián Carrón came to Uganda for the first time. "I was just looking for something to do," recalls Denis. "Inside a room like this, I saw the face of Carrón, his gaze. Then he began to speak. And when he spoke, a door opened up for me, a door in my life." George: "I still remember that gaze: it penetrated to my bones. While he spoke, I followed this gaze, and it was as if the darkness of death kept receding more and more. I felt the leap of my heart inside me again. That night I couldn't sleep; I wanted to see him again as soon as possible." So it was for the others.

But the most surprising thing came after. And George is the one who tells it: "I wanted to follow that man wherever he went. My heart leapt and felt like it was going to explode. I went to Aunt Rose and told her that I wanted to be baptized, because this was the only thing that in that moment, in my opinion, would bring me close to him." And he was not the only one: after him came another and another. After the preparation of catechesis, "we were baptized, twelve boys and girls, and here began our journey. That gaze eliminated the terror of death and filled me again with songs of joy. We asked to be helped during the School of Community and, singing, we kept understanding more. We formed the so-called Kireka Battalion, the alpine soldiers of Uganda: we sing Alpine songs, exactly like the Italians who went into battle singing. Some of us were child soldiers; we came from different situations that were very difficult, but all that was overcome by a gaze."

After the young men's testimonies, Rose speaks. And she says something is often repeated since then, because for her it was a turning point. "When Father Giussani chose Carrón as his successor, I obeyed. I did not have any problems: I trusted him and obeyed. After the death of Father Giussani, it seemed to me that my world had ended: I continued to look to his successor as the new head, and that was it. Then he came to Uganda. And all that these kids said happened." They asked for baptism, one after the other. "And I said: what the heck happened? I asked: 'Tell me, what word did he say? I was there at that encounter too, there were the Memores Domini from my house, there was the whole movement. What word did he say?' I looked at my notes, to see if he had said something about baptism. Nothing. Three days passed, and there were four, there were five who asked me the same things. Then I brought them to the office and said: 'Tell me the word, the phrase…' But, when I looked at them, they were no longer the boys I brought up. And I thought: 'After all these years that I spoke about the School of Community, I spoke about God, we baptized children and women, how does he come for thirty minutes and you realize that you haven't been baptized? What did I say? What did I talk about? What God did I announce to you?' Looking at them, they were truly different. And I asked myself: 'But is it true or not?'"

At that point, she continues, "I had to follow them. I had to learn the Alpine songs with them. When they discovered something on the internet about Father Giussani, I discovered it with them. At a certain point, I also changed my gaze. I began to follow Carrón no longer as a boss but to look at *what he was looking at*. My position changed." He was no longer a boss, but "a friend, a companion on the journey."

This shows a decisive aspect of Rose's attitude. Something that continually opens roads, keeps the treasure from rusting, the life from drying up. She accepts that she has to learn: from the kids, just as she does from the women. They are her children; she brought them forth out of nothing; she saved their lives, literally. But if she sees that they are taking an important step, she wants to be there to follow them, she needs to follow them, so that the step can become hers as well. So that it can help her to grow.

"This is the nourishment of our faith, and it is true authority as well," observes Carrón today. "Seeing what happened in those kids, she made herself their disciple. She was the authority, the head: but in that moment she affirmed the authority of those kids and followed them. Because she lives from this: from Christ, wherever and however he happens. Faith is an event that generates you continually and amazes you always more and more. If it is not sustained, supported, nourished constantly by what happens, in the end it becomes a devout memory: my thoughts, my fears, my prejudices will prevail over reality. The fact will no longer have the capacity to open a crack in a mind that is, ultimately, closed. In her, instead, it happens. Continually."

At the end of that encounter, the two thousand people in the auditorium in Rimini heard an unexpected performance: five twenty-year-olds from Kampala, plus a woman who could have been their mother, got together in a semi-circle in front of a microphone and intoned "La Montanara": "*Là su per le montagne / tra boschi / e valli d'or*" ["Up there on the mountains / among the trees / and the valleys of gold. . .]." All of it, verse by verse, until "the daughter of the sun," softly, almost whispered, to close one of the classic Alpine songs. Three minutes of applause. A few notes went their own way, but in the hall, they immediately caught the profound sense of that surreal scene: those kids are *within* what they have encountered. Identified, down to the details.

Facts like these were the impetus for a beautiful experience of CLU, the university students of CL. Together with Kenya, these form the largest group of students of the movement in Africa. They are closely helped by Europe: twinned with Spanish "colleagues" and helped by Father Nacho, who was coming yearly to preach the spiritual exercises and since 2012 has led a yearly common vacation as well.

Many of the university students are children of the women of Meeting Point. They live a life like their European friends: studies, common tables at the university to meet classmates, and School of Community, the heart of CL education. "There are two of them a week: for those who cannot come to these, we see each other on Saturday," says Repossi, who follows them closely. Seeing them in action, he observes "a paradox, above all in those who come from the Luigi Giussani schools: they are more prepared, but they often struggle." They find themselves in an environment where the professor is not readily available, questions are not acceptable, students have to keep their distance. "Whereas they have seen that there can be another way of learning. The impact is tough sometimes." And how is it for you being with the kids? You are not a professor or even a teacher. "No, but doing this work with them helps me a lot, because I realize right away when I am repeating abstract formulas and when I am speaking about my experience."

They recognize it immediately, because they are people who are already solid. "One of the most significant things that I heard Rose say in the last two years is that she is happy when a kid tells her 'no,' because it means that she is raising free people," says Nacho Carbajosa. "In Europe, you can understand the pedagogical sense of a phrase like this, but you do not catch all its potential, because our kids are used to saying 'no' often. In Africa, it is very different. With the type of education that exists here, the young people struggle to have a face in front of an adult. They tell you what you want to hear, and then they do what they want. These kids don't."

It is "a path that is a long time coming," adds Father Nacho, in which "many have suffered, a few have left. Only Fredy has remained of the Alpine singers of Kireka. But even among those who have distanced themselves, or who come and go, something has begun that you cannot measure, something remains." He speaks about Grace who had a baby boy ("she called him Baby Nacho Seve Giussani"), she left for a little, and now orbits again around the friends from before. And about Arnold, "the biggest wound for them": coming back from an encounter in Europe, he fled. He decided to remain in Brussels and requested asylum there. "But it is clear that he has a path behind him; and one cannot forget a gaze of certainty on his life."

Education is a risk. Always. It always involves freedom. "In front of a risk like this, there are those who express doubts: 'See? They need to be controlled more, you need to impose rules,'" says Father Nacho again. "Instead, the method is the same; it never changes: freedom and experience. And yet, it is not written anywhere that the path of a kid has to be linear: one maybe leaves and then returns after years, having walked the path that he needed to walk. But at that point it is his, it is his decision."

We return to this point: to Rembrandt and *The Prodigal Son*. To the embrace of Father Giussani, with his beret on his head, to Rose just coming out of Linate airport, and to the infinite multiplication, the contagion of that gaze that has been seen a hundred, a thousand, ten thousand times in the lives of these kids and their families.

"Rose for me is one of the clearest examples of what it means to follow and to be generated in a relationship of sonship," observes Prosperi. "She is totally a daughter of her history and her culture, but at the same time she is totally a daughter of Father Giussani, of this encounter that changed her life. To the point that one does not feel any forcing when one sees the experience of the movement being proposed in that context, which is culturally very different from where CL was born: there is a total immediacy, without any forcing. It is the same event, the same gaze."

It is the gaze that conquered Marvin, the brother of Clare, an imposing young man with a beautiful smile, who during lunch picks up the guitar and passes readily from U2 to Neapolitan songs to Lady Gaga: "Tell me something girl / Are you happy in this modern world? / Or do you need more? / Is there something else you're searching for?"

It is the embrace that welcomed Gladys, with short hair and brilliant eyes behind enormous glasses, who told her story in a video at the Rimini exhibit. "I am twenty years old," she said, "but it is like I began to live eight years ago." That is, when she entered Luigi Giussani High School for the first time. "On February 24th, a foundational day," she remembers. "I was born there, because I encountered an experience." Something—or someone—who helped her to overcome the weight of a childhood in which "it was not easy either to be at home or to go to school," and "I grew up hating life and myself." What happened that day? "The teacher welcomed me with a smile. In seven years of primary school, I do not remember any of my teachers smiling at me. Then she asked me my name. And she promised to help me catch up because school had already started two weeks earlier."

For her, she says, it was inconceivable. "That day I felt really loved. I felt that someone loved me without even knowing who I was. Maybe at that moment I did not realize the importance of that event, but even after years it is something that I remember with a lot of nostalgia. I was at home." Father Nacho remembers a particular detail about Gladys: "When we go to Kenya, to the vacation with the students there, we take a bus: twelve-thirteen hours of travel, in damaged vehicles. An odyssey. Once I was seated next to her. We began to talk. She was quoting entire lines of Giussani from memory, but she did it in order to tell her story."

This is the same embrace that Priscilla felt for herself. Better, "Achan Priscilla," as she introduces herself with the surname in front of her name, as they do here. She is twenty-three years old and teaches English and literature at Luigi Giussani Primary. She finished the university in grand fashion, so much so that many expected to see her become a chair in a high school soon: "But I am attracted by what happens here because I grew up in this school. I do not want to leave this beauty to go somewhere else. I want to grow with these children. If I look at my heart, I recognize that this is not less than teaching in a high school." Here, she says, she learned that "teaching is not only a way to make children happy: it is first of all a relationship. With them, with the principal, with my colleagues." In her lessons she tries to put herself in the shoes of her students, "to look at their concrete situation, one by one. I find that it is an important thing to work on as a teacher: when I enter the classroom, am I interested only in explaining my material, or do I want to know who they are? For me, it is a success when a child begins to discover himself; so many times they can do well in school but not learn anything about themselves."

You listen to her, and you hear a deep echo of Rose as well as strong accents of Giussani. They are like family resemblances that you see in a child, that make you say, "She is the daughter of . . ." even if you have another individual in front of you, with her own personality. Priscilla's personality is solid, despite a story full of difficult blows: her parents died of AIDS when she was small. Her older brother brought her and her other two brothers up (his name is Aaron, and he now works at Meeting Point, "and for me he is a hero; I know the sacrifices he has made"). She had to find a place in a hurry, just after finishing high school, because they needed money in the house. "I went to the Luigi Giussani Institute to do the cleaning." But, she says, she always had people around to help her: "I met teachers who were here for me, and they helped me understand that everything that happens is for me: it is God who makes it happen. He is a father who loves me."

She ended up in the classroom because she is clever, alert, and has a real passion for education. When Mauro Giacomazzi understood this, he spoke with Rose. Priscilla left the cleaning job to begin university and then to return to the primary school classroom while she finished her studies. In the beginning she struggled; it seemed like she could not make things go her way. But then she decided to change her tactics: together with the grammar and oral exams, she began to talk about herself and her difficult story. And this created bridges even with the most rebellious kids.

For example, Julies, who "came to school only one or two times a week; to see him in class was a miracle. From the scholastic point of view, he was very behind, and I used to look at him and think: 'He doesn't want to study, he will never make it.'" Instead, when his teacher began to speak about herself, he found in those stories something of his own: "He opened up, and I realized that he was a very intelligent boy. He had my same problems: family, money. . . . To come to school was a real sacrifice, because it meant overcoming hunger and tiredness." But he did it for one reason, and one day he told her clearly: "Teacher, this is the only place I have found someone who loves me. People look at me badly: they judge me, they think that I am a degenerate. But when I come here, I feel at peace. I only want to be loved, even with my low grades."

"Here is the education I am speaking of, not performance," explains Priscilla. "He would not have been among the best at the exam. But that moment was a success. I cannot say that I failed as a teacher." Julies now works in a bakery; he makes sweets, and he is happy. But the same happens with other kids. Like Alan, another rebel from the slum who just yesterday started crying in class. "You made me think about my dad who was killed in an accident," he said to Priscilla. "I know that I am going through a difficult time, but I understand that things can change even when you think it is impossible. And I need to change my life." She looked at him in awe, thinking: how is this possible? "I still don't know how it happened; but to share one's experience is a miracle that helps many of them." And if you ask her why it is so urgent for her that those children already wounded by life become men and women, she responds: "It is the truth of your heart to love another. And if you love someone, you desire the best for him. With kids, this is how it is. You try to help them to use their head, to judge things: this is the biggest help I can give them. To keep their heart open, not to distract it from what it is seeking. I want good for them. But it is the same good that I have received."

The same good that she lives with Rose, "who looks at me like a mother, and when I went to tell her that I wanted to do a Masters in Great Britain, instead of responding, 'Come on, how could you?' she only said to me: 'Why not?' I was left with my mouth open. And she: 'Prisci, what I desire for you is that you be happy. If to do this Masters can make you happy, I am here for you. I will always be here for you.' I remained in silence. Who gets offered a love like this?"

11

Today and Tomorrow

THERE WAS A meeting in the slum, one of the first after the Covid lockdown let up. The women were telling their story. They were looking at their experience in order to learn, as they are accustomed to do. "One of them, at a certain point, said: 'I recognize that if I were hungry, I could ask my neighbors for a cup of beans; if I were thirsty there was someone to give me a glass of water. But life? Who can I ask for life?'" Rose tells this story seated on the windowsill of the balcony at her house, under a sky that is a mix of dark clouds and rays of sunshine. She speaks about Covid, about two years that paralyzed the world. We all lived the same experience at the same time. But how many of us asked questions like that?

"I came to Kireka and Naguru and I was moved," Rose remembers. "They were helping each other. They lent each other things. You could not go out to the market, but those who managed to buy something to eat gave it to those who had nothing. There were also those who kept a basin outside the door of their house, to allow those who didn't have water to wash their hands. It seems absurd, doesn't it? You have enough for two days for you and your children and you cut them in half to give to those in need. . . . And yet, that is how it was, and I wasn't expecting it." And then that question that left her astonished, to the point that she repeats it continually: "And life?"

In Uganda, there were many left dead by Covid: by the middle of 2022, they numbered 3,600. The women often say it, laughing: "For us it is just one more virus." Maybe the numbers aren't as precise as with us, and it is probably underestimated. A beautiful positive difference is the median age of the population, much lower than in the West. The first two years of the pandemic in sub-Saharan Africa did much less damage than what was feared. The big, devastating impact was on society: heavy lockdowns, schools closed for two years in a row. Lives suspended as far as possible, in a place where life is a continual whirlwind.

This strange and lengthy moment, with rhythms slowed by the force of things and the few certainties there are up in the air, led to a kind of slow motion, making it possible to see more slowly and up close—almost through a microscope—certain aspects of life here around Meeting Point. Meetings suspended, the usual aid blocked, the gates of the schools closed: there came out more clearly not only what was lacking, but above all *what was there*, because it grew during those years. What is there are people, human subjects who are stable, strong. Stronger than the thousand difficulties that they have around them, including Covid.

At the end of the trip, this is what strikes you most from Rose's world. It forces you to overturn what you usually think about poverty and how to face it: what is decisive is not the *project*, but the *subject*. Money, organizations, aid are fundamental; they would be missed if they disappeared. Without those things, everything you see around you would not be possible. At least, not in this way. But the leverage point, the point of real change, is the person. The initiatives that work are all born from here: from a person who is changed and from a change of those who are around that person. And when these subjects are women, the revolution seems to be even more powerful. "In fact, here in Kampala, in contrast to other things you find around, you see an Africa that is becoming a protagonist," says Giorgio Vittadini, synthesizing effectively.

There is another point to reflect on: what is poverty, what is need? Is it only misery, hunger, sickness, or is it something more? "Rose herself has a clear conception of her own poverty," observes Prosperi. "We are all poor, because what we have is not ours: it is a gift, starting from our very humanity. Looking at ourselves like this, it is easier to identity with the poverty of another, that is, with the profound need to be filled by what you lack in life. And that, ultimately, is the gaze of goodness that makes you say: 'You have value. Your life has value.' For her, it is not just a consoling phrase. It is an awareness of herself that reflects on the other, whoever he is." And it changes her way of acting.

If you ask him what characterizes Rose's way of acting, in comparison with the other thousand projects that he sees in governing AVSI, Giampaolo Silvestri responds with two things: "One, the stable presence of the people. In our sector, interventions are a bit 'hit and run': you arrive, you do something beautiful, and you leave. She has been here for thirty years: she creates strong bonds, and this makes the difference. Two, she takes on a complex need that, in time, changes. She started out as a nurse: medication for those sick with AIDS, then the discovery of the value of the person, the women. But in time the need changed: the need for a school came out, and she gave herself to working for that. Then, the young people, the university. . . . They are interventions that start from needs, but also from the people's desires. The problem of AIDS, was the first need: to care for others. But the school was also a desire. She followed the desire of these women."

Desire. It is infinitely bigger, infinitely broader, than bare need. It is part of the need and animates it. And if instead of stopping at the need ("Are you hungry? Are you sick? Here is some food and medicine, or a way to make money."), you arrive at desire. If you cultivate it—if you educate it—desire explodes. It becomes an inexhaustible resource, capable of surprising even those who have always known you.

"When the lockdown ended and we began to meet with the women again, Rose was almost afraid," recalls Mónica Fontana Abad. "She said: 'Who knows what we will find, how they lived, if they have eaten. . . .' Her most fragile side came out. Instead, she came back home and was regenerated: full of their stories, of the things that had happened. The truth is that they were a help for us to live the pandemic."

This is an important indicator. "It means that through the education here something has happened," observes Repossi. "You see, many times, when people hear these facts recounted, they say: 'Okay, it's clear: Rose is there, things tend to go well for her. If she isn't there, it is impossible.' And from a certain point of view this is true: you don't find someone like Rose everywhere. But during those months of Covid, she was not there among the women, and neither were we. If they didn't stop, it means that what they see in her has become their own experience." For this reason, he adds, "the work we are doing, even with the social workers, is to try to understand together what is really there underneath, what the method is. Otherwise even they who visit the families do not grasp the essential elements. They tell you: 'Ah, I found Mary doing well, I didn't expect it: her house was clean, the little girl goes to school, they have work.' And it's over there. Instead, the question is: why? What does it mean that a woman is able to live this way even in the midst of Covid, when we are not there? What is it a sign of?"

It goes back, again, to education, which in the end is the only real occupation of Rose and of those who are around her. Of the "Covid postmen," the teachers who went around the slum on motorcycles to bring homework to the kids, house to house, as mentioned above. But it is also interesting what happened at a certain point. "After a month and a half, we asked Rose: let's meet, we want to tell you what we are seeing and discuss together certain problems," Severgnini remembers. "You go to the houses of the kids, and you see all types. We have a nice Excel file of the kids we met, the problems, and possible solutions. And we were rightly proud."

The lunch comes, the principal brings out the paper and begins: "Joe, here, has this problem. . . ." Rose, recalls Severgnini, didn't even let him finish: "She stops us and asks: 'In your opinion, how many professors are there in the world who sought out their students, one by one?' We: 'Probably very few. You know, the others do distance learning. We are so broke that we don't even have internet.' 'No, no: how many?' 'Um . . . very few.' 'For me this is a point we can't forget. We have to understand what moved your hearts to the point that you went out and found the kids. If you lose what happened in your heart, all that you do, even the solution to these problems will not last.'"

Severgnini calls it "a true judgment, which offered a newness. That lunch went, for that reason, from 'we present you problems with possible solution' to telling each other what had moved us. It was that moment that helped us recover the initial point." It was an education of the educators.

It is a work that is never completed. In some ways, it is a work that needs to begin again and again. Because there is nothing automatic about it: it engages your freedom and the freedom of the other constantly. It challenges your limits, your errors, your skepticism, your disappointments, every morning.

Rose has had plenty of disappointments, big ones too. People who refuse help and affection. People who have taken advantage of her help or have left, both the kids and even some of her closest friends; maybe in order to embrace a sect or to start something that resembled Meeting Point, but separate from it. These are wounds that in many cases are still open; but they are not scandals—that is, to use the term according to its etymology, "a stumbling block, an obstacle." In fact, "one of the things that has always struck me about her is that she has stayed in relationship with many of these people, and when she can, she continues to help them," says Silvestri. One of them, for example, is Vicky, the woman who in *Greater* told about her friendship with Rose and how she was saved by the encounter with her. She left a few years ago, she chose other paths, but now and then they still see each other. The reason is simple: Rose appeals to freedom, and freedom is something sacred. "Look, I am happy when the women or the kids tell me 'no,' even in front of beautiful things," says Rose. "It is the sign that they are growing free."

"I too, after three months, wanted to return home," says Severgnini. "I was exhausted. School had just started, and I saw problems everywhere. But not structural problems: human ones. It seemed impossible to keep up a school with people who worked like this. At a certain point I said to Rose: 'I am going back to Italy.'" And she? "She looked at me and said: 'Seve, here there are two types of expatriates: the enthusiasts who arrive to resolve all the problems of Africa, and the cynics, who are last year's enthusiasts. . . .' And it is true: when you see that your projects are only a drop in the ocean, first you think that you are not adequate, then—given your egotism—you begin to say: 'No, they are the ones who are wrong,' and you become wicked. I had spent those months passing from one extreme to the other." And how did you get out of it? "Rose added: 'I don't need someone who comes here to save Uganda. I just need someone who can say 'yes' to Jesus. The biggest contribution you can give your students is this.'" Words that Severgnini had heard so many times, "without ever believing them deep down. But I couldn't help but believe her. I said to myself: 'Okay, if I have to say "yes" to someone, I have to look for a specific face to say it to.'"

He recounts what happened afterward: "I didn't leave. I returned to school. And I began to realize that, before that dialogue with Rose, I was thinking about reality as a collection of problems to solve; afterward, reality became the possibility for a relationship with Christ. It was the means to say to him: 'Help me see. Help me see here where your face is.'" And then, he discovered three things: "One: that I spoke continually about reality but never listened to it. I saw a thing, and I applied a solution, but I did not give myself time to listen. Whereas reality speaks so much, and silence helps to listen to it. Two: I was never alone; I never had to solve problems with my own titanic effort. I had faces around me, to which, at first, I had given zero trust and that instead were there, with my same desire. We could work together. Three: I realized that I wanted to learn. I came out with so many questions: about pedagogy, education, about how to be in a classroom here in Africa. . . . And I learned."

These words are repeated in Repossi's story: "Deep down, you have the feeling that you are always going backward. It is as if the more you enter into things, the more you understand that you have not understood. You understand that reality is bigger and opens another door for you. It is a grace to be able to learn continuously from what happens. I think the beauty of being here with Rose and the women is also because that they never leave you in peace. Looking at them, you understand that even when you are at peace, that is not what you want. I am very happy. Thinking that you can always live like this, that you always need to learn, is a continual adventure."

If there is something that helps this continual restarting, it is the School of Community. It is the cornerstone of the educational method of Father Giussani and CL. Those who participate work on a text, often from Giussani himself. They read it and study it personally. And then they meet in groups, every week or two, to work together, following an invitation: to compare those words to life, to what has happened or what they are living. To reflect on their own experience and to help each other understand it, in the light of the text and of the experience of others. For Father Giussani, and those who follow him, experience is the way to verify if Christian faith responds or not to the demands of life. And this stable, methodical work on the School of Community helps to learn this verification continually.

In Kampala, Rose is the one who leads the main meeting (others are held in different places or among the university students) every Thursday afternoon, in a classroom at the Luigi Giussani Institute of Higher Education. An hour and a half without break, questions and answers, without leaving space for intellectual deviations or abstract questions (in these parts that is also less common...): only stories, facts that have happened and what people have learned from them, together.

It is striking to see Agnes in the second row, with her glasses on her nose, intent on taking notes. You remember what she said at the table at Meeting Point: "One day Rose came to me and asked: 'Shall we go to School of Community?' And I: 'What is that?' 'A meeting where we talk about life, where we learn and we understand ourselves more deeply. It will help you.' In the beginning, I said no. Then I went one time. I heard these people reading and speaking, and I was disturbed within. I thought: 'Why did Rose talk to these people about me?' What they were talking about was exactly how I was feeling: they were problems that touched my life, the desire I had. . . . I was upset. I told her: 'If I would have known, I would never have come.' But what they said stayed inside me. I recognized myself in their words. Rose only answered: 'Don't worry, with time you will understand.' And then I decided to continue going with her." In the back row is Hanifa, a Muslim woman: she does not write, but she is very attentive, to catch "that word or two that then will help me live." It is impressive to hear from Teddy phrases like "silence is important because it is the moment when you reflect on life: you can see the mystery of life, its miracles, all the problems you have passed through. The problems are still there, but you are better able to go through them. The one who is giving you the gift of life now will always take care of you; there will always be someone or something who will help you. Then my task is just to be attentive: to pay attention to the Mystery and not to take for granted what happens in life."

Julián Carrón has seen these women; he knows them well. Reflecting on that scene, he smiles: "Many have said, for years, that Father Giussani is complicated, he uses difficult words. There you see the opposite. I have never heard them say that. Because the point of departure for them is not an intellectual approach, but an experience. And with experience they have the key to enter into the text. As Saint Augustine said: *In oculis facta, in manibus codices* [In our eyes facts, in our hands texts]. The facts that happen help me to understand the texts and the texts illuminate life. When it is not like that, you stay at the level of appearances, in pure rationalism. And you suffocate. In the women, instead, you see the pertinence of faith to their needs from the gladness and the peace they have. Because they find that their lives are saved, in any circumstance."

Encounters like this one multiplied over a long period of time. It was another paradox of Covid. The exhibit of the Meeting in 2021 should have arrived the year before. They had been working on it in Kampala for a while already. After many months of work, the pandemic postponed everything until the next session of the Meeting. That work, done in groups—involving not only the women, but the students, the AVSI workers, the Memores Domini—was done with a method very similar to the School of Community of sharing stories and experiences. It ended up going far beyond the exhibit that moved so many people at Rimini, later traveling around Italy. For everyone, especially for Rose, it was the occasion to re-read their own story. For many, it was an opportunity to focus on the value of certain times of struggle as well.

"My relationship with Rose was unique," says Mónica Fontana Abad. "I had met her twenty years ago, because she had come to Spain. She gave a talk at my university. I was there, seated among the students, hearing her speak about what she always says—because in reality she says more or less the same things, but with a newness each time you hear her. It was an event. In that moment, I was not able to say why, but I found myself thinking: 'How I would love to know this woman more.'"

Twenty years later, she found herself living with her, in the house in Kampala. And she saw in front of her "a normal woman, with all the limits that we all have. It was a bit of a shock; the image that I had made of her held me back. The first year I struggled: 'Damn, I always wanted to be here, and now. . . .' Yet I saw that Rose has an affective certainty that I really want for myself."

At that time, the work for the exhibit began, and Mónica curated the catalogue (together with Severgnini): "I threw myself again into the relationship with her. I wanted to discover and learn. It was like going beyond appearances. I too at times look at myself according to a false thought, instead of for what I am. I went beyond the appearances to a recognition of who she is. And from there was born an eternal friendship; I don't know how else to describe it. She made me discover and enjoy so many things that I didn't see before."

Other friendships have experienced similar trajectories, even friendships from further away. "The bond with Rose for me was a slow path of affection," says Stefano Antonetti, a businessman. He is from Varese and is married to Manolita Salandini, the daughter of one of the doctors who first arrived here with the Fraternity in Uganda: she had already been back in Italy for years, but love for Africa is contagious. The result: they have been here since 2000, on a path that has not always been easy. "But going through it together, thanks to the work on the exhibit, was moving; and it made me understand this journey much more."

It the beginning, Antonetti recounts, there was a problem of relationships, the difference of vision, "and we were not really friends with Rose." At a certain point, in 2011, they had decided to return home. "I went to tell Rose. I expected her to say something about the circumstances of our leaving, and instead she asked me a question: 'Why?' It floored me. I thought that we were not very important to her, and instead that question put me back in motion." Manolita says that, "we had to decide again about the true reason why we were here. Which does not have to do with hanging out with friends or not. This began to dig, like a worm. Until at a certain point, I said to myself: what truly interests me in life? To fix problems, or to go to the depths in my relationship with the Lord?"

They remained. And in time the friendship with Rose grew. "She was the leader of the movement here," recalls Manolita. "And sometimes you follow because you are following 'the boss.' But little by little, it became for me the following of a friend, someone who, you understand, loves you. It became an affectionate relationship, a relationship of real belonging."

Samuele Rizzo—the one who as a child found the girl from Kampala in his house for months when she was stuck in Gulu because of the rebels—tells a similar story: "Rose doesn't have an easy character: if she has to send you to hell, maybe she doesn't say, 'Go to hell,' but she makes you understand for sure. Probably early on the relationship was marked by certain things that had happened with my father and others. But when these preconceptions fell apart, a deeper friendship began."

The exhibit was a way to recognize the depth of a moment that everyone here remembers as a leap of awareness, not to be taken for granted: the death of Francesco Frigerio, the businessman whose photo you saw on the wall at the high school. It was a difficult time for these friends. "We had to come to grips with death," says Antonetti. "But the clarity of Rose's judgment helped us to face even that fact as a part of life, not as something to censure."

The year and a half of work on the exhibit brought all this to light. There are stories like that of Marco Ponselé and Francesca Peverelli, who are younger and who came in 2020. He had come to Kampala six years earlier almost by chance; he was in Kenya working on his thesis. "I was with a friend. There was a meeting at the Institute, and we just happened to be there. Rose came to meet us and basically brought us all around for two days, visiting everything: Meeting Point, Welcoming House, her house. It struck me. I remember before leaving, at the airport, I told her: 'After this experience, I feel that something will be missing in Italy.' And she: 'What you have seen here must not be a memory to lament, but a springboard to live the same thing in Italy.'"

He met Francesca a little later, they fell in love, and when she chose to do civil service, he suggested Uganda. She came here for a year. Being with the women, she says, turned her life upside down: "I understood from them what it means to consist of a belonging. Your consistence, what you see when you look in the mirror, what you feel when you are crushed by the struggles of life, is the relationship with God. I had never seen this in the flesh. I also think about the little kids of the Welcoming House, who don't have anything. They have only third-hand underwear, but sometimes I see that they are more solid than I am. They take initiative, they have an irony, a freedom. . . . You understand that their security has an origin that cannot be explained only by what you see; there has to be *something else*. In the end, the thing that attracts you being with Rose and the others is not just them: it is their relationship with God."

When they got married, it was a clear choice to come to Kampala. They work together for AVSI. The more you are with Rose, the more you say: this gaze is capable of sustaining me for a lifetime." She recalls a fact that helped her understand: "one day there was this kid who had received fifty Euros for his birthday from a supporter in Italy. The bad idea came to Rose of taking him to the mall to pick out a gift. She wanted to buy him a backpack for school, something useful. Instead, he saw a toy car and went crazy. He started making a scene, having a tantrum.... Unthinkable, for a kid like this: they are all very well-behaved; for example, when Rose arrives with the groceries they get in a line to help her unload the car."

In front of the racks where there were three backpacks, he said: "I don't know which one to choose." "Rose gets fed up, picks up a backpack and goes to the cash register. Then we don't really understand what happened, but we saw that she told him: 'Okay, go get this toy car.' He had studied the map of the mall in order to find that toy: it took him a minute to go and come back again. Happy. When we spoke about it, Rose wanted us to understand what she had understood. 'One has a tantrum only when he feels loved. If he was afraid of the one who was watching him, he wouldn't have had the courage. That an AIDS orphan feels so loved that he has a tantrum is the defeat of the sickness.' You see episodes like this, and you think: I have never met anything that corresponds so well to how I am made. Never. Not even in a culture that is more similar to mine. When that gaze is lacking, it is difficult to live."

Who knows where the toy car is now. You ask yourself this while the white Toyota rises toward the last stage of the trip: Welcoming House. It is the house that takes in orphaned and abandoned children. "We began it in 2001," says Rose. "First, I rented a few apartments, a few rooms. But at a certain point, there weren't any more available. And so we built." There are sixty-three rooms now. "But every now and then I lose count," she laughs. "A few months ago, a policeman came with his iPad, for the census. 'Whose house is this?' 'Mine.' 'How many people live here?' I responded: 'Now, fifty-eight.' He looked surprised. And I: 'No family planning,'" and she smiles again.

By law they are all under her care. In fact, she has adopted them. "Today I was buying some baby bottles at the supermarket. Someone asked me: 'Are these for your grandkids?' And I: 'No, for my children.' He looked at me a little strangely...."

A woman who has decided not to get married and has chosen virginity, who to the question "Have you ever been in love?" answers, with a smile:

"No. Not yet. The Lord has not given me time," today she is the mother of around sixty children. From six months to twenty years old and beyond, because "we don't send anyone away from here: when they are big enough, if they want to, they can go." Welcoming them, for her, "is like the flourishing of my vocation. In the end, they grow up and choose their path. There are those who have gone to school and are working, others who have started a family. What I want is for everyone to grow up and live their lives, that's enough. I am not the one to determine their destiny. Certainly, they have one. If they are born, their destiny will be there."

We arrive at the wall with its gate. We beep so the guard can look out and open the gate. And then the car parks in an open space that a little further ahead opens into a courtyard, about a dozen meters long and twenty meters wide. A lawn, a hedge around it, two iron swings, a soccer goal. A few square meters covered by an awning in front of the entrance to the building. Seven or eight children run out, celebrating. One stops to look at the guest, astonished. But after a minute, the ball comes out, and he becomes an excellent teammate in an unexpected little.

They line up for introductions, one by one, like the women at Meeting Point: first name, last name, grade, and school. Many go to the Luigi Giussani schools. Some have extravagant names: there is a Marco Trevisan, an Alberto (like Repossi), two named Seve. They come after a generation of kids named Luigi Giussani, a few named Vittadini or Carras (after Jesus Carrascosa), and then some named Julián, a Nacho, and a Davide Prosperi. Names chosen by the mothers, when they were alive, or by Rose herself. "It might seem bizarre, but it is a way to link them to a history, to remember that they belong to a place," Silvestri says.

The two smallest do not speak; they are still in diapers. To hear all the others say "my name is" opens your heart: they were at risk of not having a story, of being nobody for nobody. And now they are there, with their proud or shy faces, and when someone puts on music, many of them begin to dance, which is another way of saying "I." Here is a place where they do not just grow up, but where they *become children*, where they gain at least a sliver of that carefree attitude that they never had, or lost too soon.

One who came who was malnourished from birth. His parents are alive, but they were not able to stay with him. They brought him to the hospital because he was throwing up, and he was discharged three days later, when their insurance money ran out. "This is how it is often done: three days without care, and they leave the same as when they entered. We took him ourselves, and now he is better; yesterday I already saw him walking around." Another arrived during the lockdown: born prematurely, he weighed only one kilogram. "He is that one there. Now he weighs twelve, and he is not even able to walk," and she points him out.

"I never tell their stories in front of them," she says softly. "I have never told many that I took them off the street. I want this to be a normal home for them, where there is someone who loves you and that's it. Sometimes you see adoptive parents, even the good ones, introduce their children like this: 'These are our natural children, that one is adopted.' The child knows that he was not born from you, but he needs to hear you say that he is yours. If he does not hear this, he does not feel at home. In time, he puts a question mark on all your love for him. I want them to be certain of this: they are loved."

We too will keep names and stories separate. But it is important to hear them. It helps us understand what it means to see them arrive here from a black hole—death, a sickness, an incurable disease—or from nothing, or almost nothing. Like what happened to one of the last ones to arrive. "We were at home with Mónica, who was still living here, and Chrispine, and we were doing yoga in the garden," says Rose. "I heard a call. 'Central Police.' I think: 'Oh God, what have I done?' But they called me 'madam,' and when they talk like this you can be calm," she laughs. "They said: 'You have to come help us, madam.' Someone had abandoned a newborn outside a house of sisters, and the sisters brought him to the police. The police know who we are, and they called me. I went to take him. And I brought him to Welcoming House." Now he is there playing there, with his baptismal name that came out of the conversation they were having during that yoga session.

A month later, another call: "Madam, there is an abandoned child." He was born premature. "The mother left him in the parking lot of the parish early in the morning, in a plastic bag. She had put two holes in the bag so he could breathe. He needed an incubator, but in the hospital at that moment, with Covid, there was no place for him. Then we used the 'kangaroo method': when mothers have premature babies, here they keep him on their skin, like a dress. At Welcoming House there was not even a bottle small enough: we had to give him milk with a spoon. And we saw his eyes after a month, because he couldn't open them. But a little bit at a time he grew. You see him now?"

The last afternoon in Kampala goes like this: dances and games and a little soccer game in the courtyard of Welcoming House, while some of the bigger kids take a break from studying. When you are short of breath, you stop, you sit. You see them go on playing. The same question arises in front of the women in Kireka: who are these kids? Why are they happy?

Rose seems to read your mind. "People today no longer know what they want," she says. "They don't know for themselves, let alone for their children." A pause. "You see, our nature is to be loved. We do not know anymore what this means, to love. It is not enough to say, 'I love you': it is something more. It is to discover that we are loved, wanted, now. My children have no doubt about the fact that I love them, even when they have a tantrum or make a mistake. They know it: they are loved. And so they know who they are."

There is a page in the Gospel where Jesus Christ says to his disciples something radical: "If you do not become like children, you will not enter the kingdom of heaven." I do not think he was talking about Paradise: it has always seemed to me that he meant "you cannot be happy today, *now*." It is one of the passages that strikes me the most. Now, maybe, I have understood why.

12

The Wave

A PHRASE of Rose, in one of our first conversations, has remained there, working under the radar. She said it in the car, coming from the slum. "Everything seems like a great wave that comes, from mother to child, and then returns back to the mother, and then comes again and every time leaves behind something more." It is true; at the end of the journey, you understand it better. All things considered, the same thing is seen everywhere: the women, the school, the encounters. A continuous job, always the same and yet different every day, and leaving at the end of the day new grains, of moving the shoreline a little further and at the same time broadening the horizon. The days go by, and the people around here grow. Not everyone and not always, certainly. There are open wounds, falls, backward steps. But in time you see a small piece of humanity that is becoming more solid, fuller. People who are more aware of themselves. And free, even in the mud of Kampala.

"It is true as well for the children, you know?" says Rose. "Sometimes, the benefactors send some extra money for a gift. You think, okay, who knows what the child will understand. But if you tell him 'you have a gift,' he comes out right away with all his freedom. He is daring. He is not afraid of the adult. The other day I told Ryan that there was a gift. And he: 'I want a moped.' I know he doesn't have anywhere to sleep at home; he doesn't even have a bed. And I tell him: 'But Ryan, I can buy you a mattress.' Do you see how the imposition is triggered, without even being aware of it? 'You are poor, therefore I will give you this. . . .'"

And Ryan?
He tells me: "well, if you cannot buy me a moped, get me a tractor." "Ryan, there is not enough money." "Then a *tuk-tuk*," you know the motorcycle vans that take people around…. It is not that they don't have problems: it is that they feel free, and they ask. They ask for something that they could probably never even ask from their mother. Someone else asked me: "Will you buy me a chicken?" They are like this, at ease, free, they ask for anything. It's like the rabbit thing.

What rabbit thing?
A few weeks ago, another gift arrived for one of the kids. He said: "I want two rabbits." I thought "fantastic," because the amount we received was exactly the price of two rabbits. And I said to myself: "Maybe he can keep them at his house.…" The day after he came and said: "My dad doesn't want any rabbits at home." Then I thought to ask Andrea, at school, if he could give us a little corner in the courtyard, to make a cage and keep them there. It is beautiful for this boy, and also for the other children. Andrea was very excited; me too. I went home with the idea that it was a job well done. They go to look for the cage and set it up. But the next day the kid comes back and says: "My dad wants to kick me out of the house. He says that I am stubborn. Instead of buying me the rabbit, can you buy me a house?" He is a child, clearly. But unless someone is free, he doesn't dare to ask you for this. So you can really say: dang, this is a success. With our own projects, many times we create a dependence, or praise for the boss. "Yes, I take good care of someone, so he gives me this." But in this way, you make the other dependent, you make him a slave. Here, that is not how things are.

And the women? Don't you ever have the impression that they depend on you?
Have you seen them? They make fun of me; they kick me [she laughs]. They are the ones who tell me, "Go here, go there." No, the women know who they are now. They too are free. And I learn with them.

But how do you make it so that, while you are trying to solve a problem, you are really serving the other and not yourself, your power over him?
When you are true with yourself, you understand because you see that what you give the other becomes constructive. Otherwise no, you hold him back. Sooner or later, you do him wrong. The other is not in your hands; he does not consist of what you give him. Man is not "what you do for him." You become aware of this only if you understand it about yourself. You are not

only what you say, you are not "what you know about yourself": you are something more. If you recognize this for yourself, you treat others in this way. And you relax.

In what sense do you "relax"?
For so long I thought that faith was "something to do." Instead, it is . . . a tranquility: it is discovering that someone is with you and loves you. That's it. If everything depended on me or on what I do, good night. . . . No, faith is first of all a problem of awareness. I do not make the Mystery. God is there, always: I am the one who so many times does not recognize him. If you reduce things, it is because you reduce yourself. Faith is not so much "what I have to do" but acknowledging that God is flesh of your flesh. When it begins to be like this, everything changes. Even your limits and your mistakes are no longer a hindrance. They hurt you, they displease you, but they are no longer a hindrance.

Why?
Because you realize that there is something greater even than the mistakes you make. There is someone who embraces everything, even your mistakes. And when you err, the error becomes a cry: you need someone to save you. Like a child playing in front of his parents. If he is alone, he is afraid of messing up. If he plays when his father is there, he is not defined by his mistakes, by falling, or by anything else. Instead, so many times, we are afraid of making mistakes and so we make even more mistakes. And when we do err, we hide it, we cover it up. You cover it up, you cover it up, and eventually you explode. You no longer distinguish between the beautiful and the ugly, the true and the false. And you no longer enjoy things. You are unbalanced. In the end, recognizing that you belong brings you this freedom: you are no longer defined by your errors but by that relationship. I consist in my relationship with the Father. And things, problems, reality, are the way to understand what this Father is saying to you about yourself, about your life. About what you are made of. Because so many times we say that "we are made by something else"; but we do not really enter into the silence that makes you say: "It is You, God, who makes me now."

This is what Father Giussani helped you discover. . . .
Yes. Immediately. One of the first times, at Corvara, he called me up. I was in another hotel. I arrived, and he was sitting down and speaking, all stirred up: "Think what a miracle, Rose: you were there in the forest, in the midst

of the crocodiles and the elephants. . . . And God took you and brought you here, to me. It is really a miracle!" And he cried; he was so moved. I was quiet, and I didn't understand. Inside I wanted to laugh: "The crocodiles? And who has ever seen them?" I had never seen an elephant. Here, if you go around, it is not like you see them on the street, and my parents didn't have enough money to take me on a safari. I didn't understand. But he saw a miracle in this, in the fact that I was there. And to me, it seemed like a hand, the hand of the Mystery that grabs you by the hair and takes you with it. And seeing Giussani cry, I said to myself: "Here there is something serious. He is seeing something else, while I am laughing." He saw everything better. He saw God. And so, he made me discover something from another world, a change of life: you are you, but you are no longer only that. You are another thing, something important. If you know it, you treat yourself differently. And you treat things differently.

What does it mean "to treat things differently"?
To discover them truly. To taste them more. Everything, even the littlest things. At table with Giussani, for example, there was nothing banal. You saw him eating a breadstick: I didn't like them, but you saw him enjoying them so much that I felt like picking one up and eating it. It is his way of doing things that attracted you, entered into you and became a part of you. It was not because "Father Giussani says so." No, you saw him and he had a fascination, a taste for things, that pulled you along. You wanted it for yourself. Everything had value; everything was precious. Beginning with me. Without this, we end up treating things badly.

That is, we don't treat them for what they really are. . . .
Well no. If you do not treat yourself for what you really are, you also treat reality for less than it really is. But, doing this, we remain empty and sad, because it seems like we are only that reduced thing. Even eating becomes only "I am hungry"; you no longer taste anything. One time there was a priest who brought some expensive fish, and Giussani sat down: "Do you see Rose? It is this kind of fish; you catch it like that. . . ." He did all these things; for him it was normal. And he communicated the infinite love of God. Infinite because it was beautiful; it was always beautiful. He was a hundred thousand times more than a father. In that gaze, you saw God who was saying: "You have an infinite value, you are mine."

And when you told him about what was happening here, what did he say?
He never asked me about my work. When I tried to talk about it, he said: "And how are you?" I said: "Fine." And I began to talk about work again. And he said again: "But how are you?" The third time I understood: "Okay, Father Gius, I understand: I am the thing that interests you, not what I do." He didn't even talk so much about God. But he was so happy that I was there, that I would never have left.

Yes, but over time problems and struggles came out. You spoke to him about them, didn't you?
Yes, but he always brought me back to the question of vocation. A few years after Meeting Point was started, we separated from the other centers, because there were certain relationships that were difficult. And Father Gius only told me this: "Don't worry. If your vocation is true, the work will even come out of the rocks." You remember when Jesus goes to Jerusalem and the Pharisees tell him: "Make these people be quiet; they are stirring up trouble," and Jesus says: "Even if I make them be silent, the rocks will begin to sing"? Like that. Giussani told me: "Let it be. If you are true with your vocation, even if you are shut up in a cage, the rocks with begin to sing." Letting go in that situation was very difficult: I had my reasons, my motivations, my projects. . . . If it had happened before those six months with Giussani, I don't know if I would have managed. But later, this is how it was: I had nothing but my vocation. The only wealth I had in the world. I left that Meeting Point and something else began, starting from scratch. And to think that after all I ended up in a place where they break rocks and sing [she laughs].

When was the last time you saw Father Giussani?
Before he died, I went to meet him, and I was a little upset. He told me: "Rose, you have to read three Psalms," and he looked in the drawer. "You have to read them." He looked, but he couldn't find them. "I will send them to you." He didn't manage to send them. I never knew what Psalms they were.

And when you think about him now?
My heart beats fast, because it is as if there wasn't any separation. It is not idolatry, God forbid. For me he was never an idol, and I have never had the myth of the "boss"; I have always kept far away from bosses. And he, if I had told him, "Father Gius, you are Jesus for me," he would have chased me down and kicked my ass [she laughs]. No, it is really that "what about God". . . . It is that through Father Giussani God took hold of me. He chose something

that was nothing, and he kept it with him. This is the genius of the Mystery: he uses the hand of another to come and get you. He used Tiboni: Tiboni grabbed me and brought me to Father Giussani. And Giussani saw everything in the light of the Mystery, even you who were in front of him. He did not preach: he saw the Mystery that was making you in that moment. It was the same gaze that I saw later, in Carrón.

In what sense?
For me, Carrón is much more of a friend, a brother. There were so many times when we had problems. One year, we were short twenty to thirty thousand dollars for the schools, and I wasn't sleeping at all. Then he came to Africa. I thought about all his responsibilities, and I asked him: "What do you do when you can't sleep?" And he: "And why should I not sleep? You have to sleep, so you don't get sick. When you wake up, it is Christ who wakes you up, who is giving you being." It is true: when I sleep, it is with him that I sleep; when I wake up, it is he who turns back to my awareness, my heart, everything. And so, I began to sleep again even in the midst of problems. What I saw in Father Giussani, I saw again in Carrón: he always sent me back to that Mystery.

But for many "that Mystery," God, remains something distant, abstract. . . .
If you start from yourself, from your experience, you understand that it is not like that. In my opinion, many times, when we say that "we are nothing," we are not going to the depth to see this nothingness. We say it just to say it. But think about when you sleep. The psychologists say that while you are sleeping deeply, awareness detaches, the body detaches from you. It is as if you were dead, in a certain sense. Then you wake up because someone, in the morning, reconnects you. He blows the breath of life in you and says: "Live." He gives you being, and you begin to live. One time, a few years ago, I got out of bed and my head started to spin; it seemed like I was in a centrifuge. I had to hold onto the furniture so I didn't fall down. The doctor told me that something had happened to the fluid in my ears. The day before, I had taken a trip on a bus, all potholes and bumps. I came home and felt fine, but evidently it affected me later. So I stayed in bed and thought: look at you, the fact that you walk, that you get up to do your work. . . . We take everything for granted. And when something forces us to recognize that it is not taken for granted, that we are made by Another, we get upset, we get depressed. Instead, it is as if someone said to you: "Look, without me you can do nothing." In the

morning, when I open my eyes and see that I exist, I breathe, I put my feet on the ground, and I recognize that I am still alive. From this, true prayer begins. It is to say "Thanks." Thanks, because I live. I live! There is nothing else. There is coffee here, and I see that I am able to drink it: I could not be able to. I take a step: who guarantees that I will be able to do that later? There is someone who loves me, to the point that he makes me live now.

This is something, in one way or another, that the women are certain about: it seems like their strength comes from there, from this "you have value because you are loved...."
But I also learn it from them, continuously. To look at them, or the young people, or the children, is a continual conversion.

What is education for you?
The discovery of the self. To help the other discover himself. If it is not that, nothing sticks. You drown the other.

And why do you insist so much on belonging?
Because, originally, we all belong. If we don't start from there, we don't build anything. If everything does not start from the origin that you have and that you are, there is only a void. You don't have any ground to plant your feet on. You only have an abyss where, in time, you will fall. Instead, man belongs. And in fact, you see that belonging liberates. If you have a point to which you can say "mine," you have a point that defines you, that identifies you. But so many times, we walk without this point. In this way, things slip into the void, into nothingness. And then we remain outside ourselves. Our imbalance and our unfulfillment come from there. Because if someone does not belong, he lacks balance. And so many times you grasp here and there, you go after things, but over time you remain empty. When you look at these women, you see it: they belong to each other. Just as they are, with all the errors and disagreements among them, but the one cannot live without the other. When someone is not there, they look for her. This belonging points to something that is more stable, that lasts in time. If not, we build things without having ground to stand on. If I did not have a place where I belong—the Church, the movement of CL—to lead these women to myself would truly mean to kill everything. It would be something that could not last in time; in the end it would be a swindle. And instead, it is this hand that has taken me and takes that other one as well, and that other one, and even the one I don't know,

even the taxi driver who came to pick me up this morning. He is made by a hand that is also making you, now.

And why does this make you free?
Because without this original relationship, we can never talk about freedom. I finally became free when I discovered that I belong, when this belonging became a face that had a first and last name. If not, I would not be free. And instead, I can say, "Now I'm free," like the women sing. And it is not just a song, but the truth of myself. You can cry, freely. You can laugh, freely. In fact, you saw how they laugh wholeheartedly. . . . But in this way, everything becomes more. Even justice, for example. It becomes a more beautiful justice. It is not only what the world says: it is much more. It is a justice that makes you feel at home.

And yet these women live continually in a condition of deep injustice.
It is true. Many of them have undergone and undergo injustices: from their sickness, from the rebels. . . . Yet you see that they are free. Which means that with everything they have lived—many people have violated them, have treated them badly and still treat them badly—they have found a justice that is even greater than what we can imagine. They are not imprisoned by their problems, by poverty, by sickness. Do you remember the woman we came across this morning? That little thing, always happy. . . . When I entered into her little house the first time, I said to myself: "O God, this woman really sleeps here?" She lived in a hole. I asked: where do your children sleep? "Here, on the mat." And she laughed; she didn't complain. But while she said it, I was dying inside. Moreover, she always wears white. Where she keeps these dresses and how she doesn't get them dirty, I don't know. Then I said to myself: all the complaints that I make are an injustice, not a justice. When it rains, water gets in the house. And yet she is free, even from injustice. How is it possible?

Does it still happen that you are moved like this? You have lived here with these women for thirty years; certain things you see again and again: isn't there a risk of getting used to it?
Yes. But the truth is that if you are not moved, you do not move. You do things mechanically, and in time you get fed up. While if you are moved, even if you err and do something foolish, you always start again. Because you see the other who is suffering, and you would like her not to suffer. You want

the other not to die. But it is not something sentimental: it is a question of knowledge.

In what sense?
You want to take her and say: "If you knew what you truly are, what reality truly is. . . ." You want to shake her. To say: "Look, things are greater than you can imagine." You desire for her to know where she comes from, for her not to reduce herself. When you find a woman who reduces herself, who does evil, it is terrible. And then you are moved: you want that woman to exist, you want her to be treated well. It is something that comes over you from within; it is not that you invent it: when you see something that is not right, you want to change it. In the end, it is still that desire for justice that we spoke about before.

Do you feel it very strongly, this desire for justice?
Yes. All the time. Everywhere. Either for myself or for others. But when you feel this desire burning within, it is a call to see if true justice, the kind that really frees, exists or not. It is the time to discover if it is true that justice became flesh. This injustice doesn't happen only because someone offended you, treated you badly. It happens so that you can recognize justice made flesh. Because in the end, Christ is justice. You cannot expect justice from a man like yourself. Even if he does justice according to the law or morality, it is very important, certainly, it is essential: but it is not enough for you. Because you are a cry for justice, a need for truth. And the other man is not capable; he doesn't have any capacity to do justice for you. He cannot do it. Even if he sets out with the best intentions, he can never fulfill that need.

But do you ever suspect that God has made a mistake? You see sickness, pain, suffering, all the time. . . .
That God made a mistake? No, I never think this. I know that what he does has its reason; he does it for a greater reason. I have never doubted the things done by God. Sometimes I fight with him: "Why did you do it like that?"

That's what I meant.
This? Yes, many times. I ask him: "Why this, why that?" Or: "This one here, what did you create him to do?" Sometimes I conclude: "Okay, now you do it; arrange things yourself!" [she laughs]. In fact, I say it often, ask him to arrange things. When I am really upset, I tell him: "You take care of things a little, with your people. . . ." And then I laugh at myself.

Do you ever feel alone?
Before Father Giussani, yes. Now I feel lonely when people do not understand what is going on. But it is not so much that I feel alone.... It is that I am displeased, that I am upset when the other does not treat herself according to how she is made and maybe ruins her life. But I understand that if God is not mine, he cannot become anyone around me. It is not that I can expect the other to understand so that I can live. I live. What the other is made of will be revealed when God wants. In the end, all these years of the journey have helped me understand that I am never truly alone. Even if at certain times it seems like Jesus is asleep, like he doesn't hear....

When, for example?
When so many people die around me. When I do not understand that justice became flesh, and I expect it from another: "They are doing this injustice to me, that one did this to me." I stop there. Like this war in Ukraine.... In the end, it is something that makes you cry out: "Where are you?" Where is God? We can make judgments, analyze this and that. But the only thing for us to understand is: where is God? Where? Because even there he is saying something to us.

Have you ever been scammed?
By certain people I thought were my friends, many times [she laughs]. And I continue to get taken. But in time you see that you are not defined by that. The other day, for example, there was this kid. He finished his exams, but he never got the results. You have to pay a state fee to get them. So I called him and said: "Okay, how much money do you have now? Bring it to the secretary, then I will pay whatever you still need." He went, got his results, and left. Disappeared. I called him: "Where are you?" "Ah, now I am walking, I don't have time," and he hung up. But, you see, even that is beautiful.

Why?
Because you think: "Okay, I did it: now he will come running...." And damn, he doesn't come. No, no, it is not that your tricks work. But I am happy about it. Because then there is nothing to get puffed up about. "I did a beautiful job." No, truly the Mystery always invited us not to get elated about the outcome, the payback. Where you expect payback, not even a little bit comes back, even if you did a good job. It doesn't come back. Instead, when you weren't expecting anything, something comes out. Why get puffed up? It is like that passage in the Gospel, remember? Jesus sends his disciples to the villages,

they come back a little later all excited because they can do miracles and even the demons obey them, and he tells them this: "You must not rejoice about this. Rather, rejoice that your names are written in heaven." Don't get excited about what you are able to do, but rather get excited because you are loved by God. One time, when Carrón was the head of CL, I went to him with a list of problems: the boss here, the leader there, the one who was putting a stick in the wheels.... He laughed, took the paper and said: "Now, let's start from the beginning. Does this person really act like this and create problems? What does it matter? What does he take from you? You are full. If you already have a full glass, what does it take from you if the other tries to fill his own? Let it go. When he realizes that you drink and are happy, he will change...." We looked at the list of problems like this. And the paper ended up in the trashcan. Because it is true: in the end, if your heart is full, if you are affectively certain, fulfilled, what do the crumbs matter to you?

And do you have "a full heart"?
Yes. Truly. I am poor, but I can say that my treasure in this world is my vocation. A little like at the beginning: I don't have anything important to give, I have only my nothingness. But if there is something for which life is worth living, it is Christ. If anything is worth giving yourself, acting, rejoicing, suffering... it is for this. I don't have anything but this.

Notes

1. Professor of Theology at The Catholic University of the Sacred Heart in Milan, Italy.
2. Luigi Giussani, cited in Alberto Savorana, *The Life of Father Giussani*, Rizzoli, Milano, 2013, p. 489.
3. Romano Guardini, *L'essenza del cristianesimo* [*The Essence of Christianity*], Morcelliana, Brescia, 1981, p. 12, Our Translation.
4. This is the proper name of Rose's association, not to be confused with Meeting Point Kampala and others present in Uganda, as we will see shortly.
5. AVSI, an international NGO present in thirty-nine countries, has fostered the birth and the growth of Meeting Point International as an independent organization that can sustain Rose's activities over time. It has helped insert thousands of children and young people from the slums into their program of distance adoption, as well as finance the construction of schools, and has sent three people from its staff to provide assistance both at the schools and at the MPI.
6. The first biography on Tiboni has just come out: Filippo Ciantia, *Padre Tiboni. Uno dei piu santi uomini che abbiamo* [*Father Tiboni. One of the holiest men we have*], Itaca, Castel Bolognese 2022.
7. All of Rose's interventions at the Rimini Meeting can be found on the site of the event: https://www.meetingrimini.org/en/personaggi/businge-rose-en/.
8. E. Castelli, *La difficile speranza*, Jaca Book, Milan, 1986.
9. This is a prayer composed by Tiboni and diffused throughout the CCL communities in those years.
10. Alberto Savorana. *The Life of Father Giussani*.
11. Luigi Giussani. *L'avvenimento cristiano. Uomo, Chiesa, mondo* [*The Christian event: Man, Church, World*]. BUR, Milan 2003, p. 32 (translation ours).

Notes

12 Lucio Brunelli and Gianni Cardinale, "Memores Domini," https://english.clonline.org/archive/altro/memores-domini.

13 Renato Farina, *Good morning, Kintu!* in *Tracce*, n. 4, 1996, p. 18.

14 Https://www.pellegrinaggio.org/pellegrinaggio/messaggie testimonianze/978t estimonianzadirosebusingyeuganda. Translation ours.

15 Ilaria Schnyder von Wartensee, Elizabeth Hlabse, Gabriella Berloffa e Giuseppe Folloni, "The role of personal identity in human development," *The European Journal of Development Research*, vol. 31, 2019, p. 461.

16 The School of Community is one of the fundamental educational instruments for those who follow CL. It consists in a reading and personal meditation on a text proposed to the whole movement, followed by communal meetings.

17 Paolo Perego, *Adesso vogliamo Tutto [Now we want Everything]*, in *Tracce*, n. 7, 2011, p. 62.

Acknowledgments

The story you have read would not exist without Father Giussani. He was born just over a hundred years ago, on 15 October 1922. This book, ultimately, is a small homage to a life that continues to generate life.

I cannot end without thanking Rose first of all: her friendship and the hours we spent together have a value for me that goes infinitely beyond these pages.

Then, "her" women: I feel that they are companions on the journey. To embrace them is a way to embrace everything that lives around them.

I thank the friends who welcomed me in Kampala, all of them, one by one. You have seen their names little by little throughout this story. I will always have their faces stamped on my heart.

I am also aware of all those who agreed to tell me about themselves and their bond with Rose. You have also met them along the way. To the friends that worked on the exhibit "You are a Value" goes one more "thanks": to have had access to the preparatory material was a great help.

I am thankful to Alessandra Stoppa and Alberto Savorana for their precious suggestions in the revision stage. And to Lucio Lorenzi for the way he accompanied the whole process.

A particular thanks goes to Julián Carrón who in many ways is at the origin of this project.

And finally, to my wife and my children. As always, I don't speak about them in the book, but they are there. On every page.

This book was set in Arno Pro, designed by the American typographer, Robert Slimbach, for Adobe Systems. Named for the river that runs through Florence, Italy, Arno Pro is a contemporary adaptation of type styles that flourished at the height of the Renaissance Humanist movement.

This book was designed by Shannon Carter, Ian Creeger, and Gregory Wolfe. It was published in hardcover, paperback, and electronic formats by Slant Books, Seattle, Washington.

Cover photographs courtesy of Meeting Point International.

www.ingramcontent.com/pod-product-compliance
Lightning Source LLC
Chambersburg PA
CBHW021201100426
42735CB00046B/805